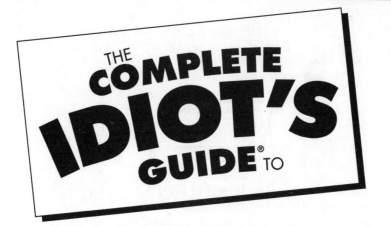

THE
COMPLETE
IDIOT'S
GUIDE® TO

The American Accent

by Diane Ryan

ALPHA

A member of Penguin Group (USA) Inc.

ALPHA BOOKS

Published by the Penguin Group

Penguin Group (USA) Inc., 375 Hudson Street, New York, New York 10014, USA

Penguin Group (Canada), 90 Eglinton Avenue East, Suite 700, Toronto, Ontario M4P 2Y3, Canada (a division of Pearson Penguin Canada Inc.)

Penguin Books Ltd., 80 Strand, London WC2R 0RL, England

Penguin Ireland, 25 St. Stephen's Green, Dublin 2, Ireland (a division of Penguin Books Ltd.)

Penguin Group (Australia), 250 Camberwell Road, Camberwell, Victoria 3124, Australia (a division of Pearson Australia Group Pty. Ltd.)

Penguin Books India Pvt. Ltd., 11 Community Centre, Panchsheel Park, New Delhi—110 017, India

Penguin Group (NZ), 67 Apollo Drive, Rosedale, North Shore, Auckland 1311, New Zealand (a division of Pearson New Zealand Ltd.)

Penguin Books (South Africa) (Pty.) Ltd., 24 Sturdee Avenue, Rosebank, Johannesburg 2196, South Africa

Penguin Books Ltd., Registered Offices: 80 Strand, London WC2R 0RL, England

International Standard Book Number: 978-1-59257-918-1
Library of Congress Catalog Card Number: 2009926600

11   10   09   8   7   6   5   4   3   2   1

Interpretation of the printing code: The rightmost number of the first series of numbers is the year of the book's printing; the rightmost number of the second series of numbers is the number of the book's printing. For example, a printing code of 09-1 shows that the first printing occurred in 2009.

Printed in the United States of America

Note: This publication contains the opinions and ideas of its author. It is intended to provide helpful and informative material on the subject matter covered. It is sold with the understanding that the author and publisher are not engaged in rendering professional services in the book. If the reader requires personal assistance or advice, a competent professional should be consulted.

The author and publisher specifically disclaim any responsibility for any liability, loss, or risk, personal or otherwise, which is incurred as a consequence, directly or indirectly, of the use and application of any of the contents of this book.

Most Alpha books are available at special quantity discounts for bulk purchases for sales promotions, premiums, fundraising, or educational use. Special books, or book excerpts, can also be created to fit specific needs.

For details, write: Special Markets, Alpha Books, 375 Hudson Street, New York, NY 10014.

Publisher: *Marie Butler-Knight*
Editorial Director: *Mike Sanders*
Senior Managing Editor: *Billy Fields*
Acquisitions Editor: *Karyn Gerhard*
Development Editor: *Julie Coffin*
Production Editor: *Kayla Dugger*

Copy Editor: *Tricia Liebig*
Cover Designer: *Rebecca Harmon*
Book Designer: *Trina Wurst*
Indexer: *Tonya Heard*
Layout: *Brian Massey*
Proofreader: *Mary Hunt*

Contents at a Glance

Contents

Introduction

Do you know what sets human beings apart from every other species on the face of the earth? We're the only ones who could come up with an advanced linguistic system to communicate with one another. We can't take personal credit, of course. We owe it all to evolution. After our predecessors figured out a way to express an infinite variety of thoughts and ideas verbally, we took one colossal leap away from whatever else was swimming in the sea, crawling on the ground, or swinging from the trees. This amazing ability that we call language comes standard with all human packages, but the variety you speak depends on where you were born and where you grew up. It's a remarkable gift that we all share.

Though we are gifted in so many ways, human nature is filled with many dichotomies. We all want to be distinctive and recognized for our individual achievements, yet we crave acceptance by the group. When we walk into a room, we're thrilled when heads turn to acknowledge our presence. Yet if our speech or accent calls attention to itself, it can be awkward or embarrassing for both the speaker and the listener. Strange phenomenon, don't you think? Because my background is in speech and language pathology and not psychology, I can't tell you why that's so—I just know that it is.

In a perfect world, this book wouldn't be necessary. We would simply accept one another's differences, and everyone would learn to adapt. But that's not the way the world is—at least not in the language department. Regardless of where we live in the world, if our accent is not like that of the majority, we want to perfect it to sound more "native." It's not a totally American issue, of course. There are books on how to speak French like a Parisian and more than likely there are publications in your own native country that help non-natives speak your language accent-free.

As you look through the pages of this book, you will see that there's quite a bit of work ahead of you. But don't panic. This book includes all the problem sounds for all those who want to improve their American English accent. In all likelihood, you have only a few sounds on which you need to focus. Will reducing your accent involve work? Of course. Unfortunately, there is no miracle spray to do the job for you. And that reminds me …

A few years ago, my husband and I decided to take advantage of his dual citizenship and move to Ireland for a year. Before we left, our friends gave us a bon voyage party and a gag gift of "Instant Irish Accent Breath Spray." After we set up housekeeping in an authentic Irish cottage in a small village on the Irish Sea, we began to make quite a few new friends. In the pub one night—how else do you make friends?—I brought out the spray to display to the group. Our new friends responded by pretending to use it themselves and spoke like it had the opposite effect on them, imitating Brooklyn taxi drivers.

In lieu of a miracle spray, this book will help you develop a realistic plan that will actually work. You'll learn the steps you need to take to sound more American, and you'll learn how to find time to practice, regardless of how busy a schedule you have.

How to Use This Book

The Complete Idiot's Guide to the American Accent is divided into four parts, each covering an aspect of American English and how you can make it work for you.

Part 1, "Finding Your American Voice," answers all the basic questions you have about accents and dialects and why it may be a good idea to modify yours. You'll begin to discover what the standard American English accent actually is, learn the differences between intonation and pronunciation, and find practice strategies that fit into your daily routine. Plus you'll even have opportunities to listen to the American English accent and record your own speech sample to see how it compares.

Part 2, "Capturing the Melody of American English," is the most critical part of the book. Although many people focus on individual sound difficulties, you may be surprised to learn that your non-native accent will improve much more quickly when your primary focus is on changing your intonation. In this part you will undergo an intonation "makeover" and you will see how much the quality of your speech really does improve.

Part 3, "Pronunciation: Consonant Troublemakers," pretty much speaks for *itself*. In this part we discuss how speech is actually produced and take a look at some of the more troublesome consonants that may be getting in your way. We'll examine each sound individually and work on ways to make producing them easier. As far as those *really* vexing sounds, I'll devote special attention to them with audio exercises that you can repeat and master. The more you hear correct sounds, the faster they will become part of your own conversational speech.

Part 4, "Pronunciation: Challenging Vowels and Diphthongs," focuses on specific sound categories that may be different from those in your native language. We look at them all, one at a time, and tell you exactly what you need to do to make them sound similar to American English.

In addition, you'll find the following:

Appendix A defines some of the words used in this book that may not be part of your regular vocabulary.

Appendix B provides a script that you can record to evaluate how close your speech is to the American accent. This sample contains all the sounds of American English so you'll have an ideal opportunity to test yourself and see how much work you need to do.

Appendix C lists common sound errors according to your native language.

Appendix D provides sources that can make the job even easier for you, along with some references used to gather information for this book.

Extras

Throughout this book, you'll find sidebars that offer tips, cautions, and other tidbits of information.

def•i•ni•tion

Once in a while, a technical word may arise that needs some additional clarification. We've cleverly entitled this box accordingly.

Info-Nugget

Looking for an interesting fact on the subject of American English for your next cocktail party? These tidbits are just fun to know.

Stumbling Block

There could be some issues that rise up and get in the way of reaching your goal. These notes will alert you when one is about to rear its ugly head.

 Sound Advice

Check these boxes for tips and tactics to help you reach your goal as smoothly as possible.

About the CD

A book about improving your accent becomes a much more valuable resource when it contains not just words but actual audio examples. I've included many audio illustrations, sound demonstrations, and practice exercises.

Acknowledgments

Completing a project such as this was a much greater task than I thought it would be. It would have been impossible without the editors of Alpha Books, especially Karyn Gerhard, who treated me as if I were the only author she was assigned to; and to artist extraordinaire Carolyn Barcomb, whose patience is beyond belief. Also deserving of my gratitude is Technical Editor Sheri Summers, who checked and double-checked my work. A major salute goes to Julie Coffin, my Development Editor, who knew as much or more about the subject as I did. Most of all, I thank my husband, Bob, for his love and encouragement and for taking on more than his share of the daily workload so I could accomplish this project.

Special Thanks to the Technical Reviewer

The Complete Idiot's Guide to the American Accent was reviewed by an expert who double-checked the accuracy of what you'll learn here, to help us ensure that this book gives you everything you need to know about reducing your accent. Special thanks are extended to Sheri Summers.

Trademarks

All terms mentioned in this book that are known to be or are suspected of being trademarks or service marks have been appropriately capitalized. Alpha Books and Penguin Group (USA) Inc. cannot attest to the accuracy of this information. Use of a term in this book should not be regarded as affecting the validity of any trademark or service mark.

Part 1

Finding Your American Voice

Some people have a gift for languages. Obviously, you're one of them. Not only do you speak your native tongue, but you have an excellent grasp of the basics of the English language as well. That's no small feat. But where do you go from here? Well, by the mere fact that you're reading this, it's obvious that you are not satisfied with the way things are. Perhaps if your accent were less obvious, you'd land that job you're after or climb the corporate ladder faster. Why, modifying an accent can even change your personality! Yes, it's true, according to one former student who told me that he was shy and retiring until he began to work on his heavy Austrian accent. And to this day—even though his American accent is far from perfect—his communication skills are flawless. It gave him the confidence to go for his dream. He gave up his body-building career, took up acting, married into the most prominent family in America, and successfully ran for the governorship of California. (Well, maybe this isn't completely true, but it helps to make my point.)

Regardless of what reasons you have to modify your accent, you're in exactly the right place to make change happen. But of course you have questions and concerns. And that's what Part 1 is all about. I discuss the practical and emotional issues that are involved in reducing your accent, help evaluate your own accent, and identify the areas that are troublesome for you. Finally, I assist you in developing a plan to achieve your goal.

Chapter 1

Building a Sound Foundation

In This Chapter

- ◆ Learning what an accent is
- ◆ Comparing an accent to a dialect
- ◆ Finding the on-off accent button
- ◆ Thinking about your accent as an asset

Congratulations on making the decision to modify your accent. You may have been thinking about it for some time. I'm glad to see you took action. By choosing to modify your non-native accent, you'll no longer be hindered by communication obstacles that may have been troubling you. Yes, it will be work, but what worthwhile challenge isn't?

Why you've made the decision is not that important. What's essential is that you've decided that you'd like to take your spoken communication to another level. In Chapter 1, we examine some important basics, deal with some personal issues, and start building the groundwork that will get you where you're going.

What Is an Accent?

Exactly what is an accent? Broadly stated, it's the way a person sounds when speaking a particular language. Someone is said to have a non-native or "foreign" accent when the sounds, rhythms, and intonations of his native language are carried over into a second language. That means that if you were born in Spain, France, Mexico, China—or just about anywhere outside the United States—your speech will be perceived by native-born American English speakers as being accented. It also means that when I visited Paris and used my college French to ask directions to the Eiffel Tower, I was the one who had the foreign accent.

Info-Nugget
Children adapt to the nuances of language early in life. If a child is not regularly exposed to a second language between the ages of 3 and 7, he or she will speak that language with an accent.

But let's dig a little deeper. Why are there so many accents? It's because there are so many languages, and each is different. Not all languages contain the same sounds; some are more nasal than others and some are more monotone. Each language has its own intonation pattern, and none of them compares to standard American English.

Accent vs. Dialect

There is another kind of accent—some linguists call it a dialect, or regional accent—and it's the way a group of people speaks its native language. A dialect is determined by where people live and the social groups to which they belong. Those who live in close contact with one another grow to share a way of speaking that differs from the way other groups in other places speak.

Let's use me as an example. I was born in New York City, in the Bronx, to be exact. As you might expect, I developed a strong New York accent—or dialect—growing up. As a child, that was fine with me. Everyone spoke like I did and I had no idea that I even had an accent. (By the way, most Americans think an accent is something that every-one *else* has.) I ran into trouble, however, when I moved to a different part of the country to attend college. People were constantly inquiring where I was from, asking me to repeat myself, and imitating my words. (Sound familiar?) It was frustrating and annoying—but it also motivated me to major in speech and language pathology, where I learned how to eliminate my accent. (Although my husband says it comes back to haunt me whenever I've had one sip too many of wine.)

What most people aren't aware of is that everyone has some kind of accent, and none of them is bad; they're just different. How you speak simply depends on where you were born, where you have lived, and who is listening to you. If English is not your native language and you speak to a native-born American, your accent will stand out. If you were born in Madrid and moved to Barcelona, your accent would be noticed. If you were born in Charleston, South Carolina, spent a few years in Dallas, Texas, and were planning a move to Boston, Massachusetts, take an interpreter with you. Just joking, of course. But we do pick up additional accents along the way. So it is possible for your speech to have traces of several different dialects.

 Stumbling Block

One of the primary stumbling blocks for non-native speakers of English is that many European and Eastern languages have only five vowel sounds. By contrast, vowels and vowel combinations in English create more than twice that many vowel sounds.

Why Change Your Accent?

Chances are you have a strong grasp of the English language. In fact, working on modifying your accent without having a solid understanding of English grammar would be like creating the frosting for a cake when you don't know the ingredients for the cake itself. But even though you may be skilled in the rules of English grammar and usage, your pronunciation and intonation patterns may interfere with your ability to make yourself clearly understood. If your accent is particularly strong, you may give the impression that you don't have a grasp of the subject you're discussing—even if you have multiple Ph.D.s to prove that you do.

In a utopian society, not having a standard American accent wouldn't matter at all. Your existing accent would be just fine. But in a world in which everyone makes snap judgments, you need to have every advantage on your side. Studies have shown that people form opinions of one another first by how they look and second by what they say. And when a person speaks with an accent that is not customary, listeners pay less attention to what is being said; rather, they focus on the manner in which it is spoken.

Of course, making the decision to modify an accent is an entirely personal one. No one can tell you if or why you should change your accent. Maybe you're not even sure it's worth the effort and are just researching the possibility. If that's the case, I'd like you to try this little exercise—and think about what your life would be like if you didn't have an accent. Close your eyes and envision the possibilities. If you see yourself in a better place—figuratively or literally, personally or professionally—then you don't need my advice as to what you should do.

Sound Advice

Don't set the bar too high. Work on improving your intelligibility, not eliminating your accent. As long as you can be clearly understood, an accent can make you more interesting, and even intriguing, to the average American.

Putting Yourself to the Test

Of course, you might think it's silly that I am asking you to analyze your motivation after you've already purchased the book. But just because this book is in your hands doesn't mean you're going to take action and complete what's necessary to reach your goal. So consider this as a motivational exercise to reinforce your decision. The questions that follow are based on reasons my clients decided to move forward.

If you answer *yes* to more than half of the following questions, it's time to get to work!

1. Do you ever feel frustrated when you speak?

2. Are you often asked to repeat yourself?

3. Do you resort to spelling rather than speaking certain words?

4. Do you feel your accent has ever kept you from performing your job to the best of your ability?

5. Do you feel that your accent has limited your career possibilities?

6. Do you prefer e-mail instead of the telephone?

7. Do you feel uncomfortable leaving voice-mail?

8. Do you avoid speaking to strangers in social situations?

9. Do you shy away from speaking in large groups because you feel you will not be understood?

10. Do you ever feel that listeners are impatient with you because of your accent?

Cultural Sensitivity

Some non-native English speakers have confided to me that they are reluctant to change their accent because they're afraid they may lose their identity or even betray their culture. If you relate to those concerns, you should know that it is entirely possible to maintain your unique cultural identity while eliminating the obstacles that your accent presents.

The skills you will learn from accent reduction will not permanently eradicate the traces of your native speech and language. In fact, the skills you learn can be turned on or off at will! Your natural way of speaking will remain in your brain, ready for action when called upon. That means it will be completely up to you when you want to speak in your native style or when you want to speak "more American." Compare it to being an actor on the stage. When the curtain goes up, use whichever accent pleases the audience most.

Realistic Goals and Expectations

In all honesty, I need to tell you that most non-native speakers of English never completely eliminate their accent, regardless of how hard they try. If you have a very strong non-native accent and your goal is to land a job as a network anchor on the national news, then you need an accent reduction program that is far more stringent and comprehensive than this one. Plus you need some one-on-one training. But if you simply want to be better understood, to reduce the number of times you are asked to repeat yourself, and to be more confident in your public speaking ability, then you're in the right place. Your goals are realistic—and achievable.

But allow me to point something out that you may not have considered. Remember that an accent adds a unique touch to your personality, makes you more intriguing to the average American, and conveys the fact that you speak more than one language. Most Americans can't.

Think of all the stars of stage, screen, and politics who have non-native English accents. Everyone recognizes the fact that they were not born in the United States, but because they have perfected their communication skills and worked to modify their accents, they are easily understood. Their accents don't get in the way of their message. In fact, it could very well be because of their accents that people pay even more attention to what these "stars" have to say. So if you look at it that way, your accent is an asset!

How Long Will This Take?

According to behavioral research, it takes about three weeks for any newly learned skill to become a habit. That means that if you are having difficulty with one particular sound and learn how to produce it correctly, you would need to use it consistently in your speech for the next 21 days for it to become habitual. As you know, you can't break a habit overnight. You can't throw a habit out the window—as Mark Twain said, you have to coax it "downstairs a step at a time."

Stumbling Block

If you gauge success by the calendar, you will set yourself up for failure. You need to realize that improvement will happen gradually as long as you stick with your plan.

Because changing your accent involves working on a number of levels, I will be coaxing you down several different staircases throughout this program. When you reach the bottom of one, you may have to climb another and start down again. How long this will take depends on a number of variables: how heavy your accent is, how strongly motivated you are, and how adept you are at learning new things.

But my advice is this: don't gauge success by the calendar. After all, you've been speaking in your current manner for quite some time. If you are serious about reducing your accent and are committed to practicing what I preach, you will see improvement. I guarantee it. Will the entire process be difficult? Certainly it will be much less difficult than learning English—and probably much easier than you think.

Sound Advice

Children who were introduced to a second language during their first five years of life read earlier, exhibit advanced reading skills, and score twice as high on language tests than their mono-lingual peers. Share the gift of your native language!

The Least You Need to Know

♦ A non-native accent occurs when the sounds and rhythms of a native language are carried over into a second language.

♦ A dialect is the way a group of people speaks its native language.

♦ It takes 21 days for a practiced behavior to become habit.

♦ After you learn a different way of speaking, you can still choose to revert to your native accent.

♦ An accent makes you distinctive and interesting and could become an asset to you both personally and professionally.

Chapter 2

Playing It by Ear

In This Chapter

- ◆ Discovering the standard American English accent
- ◆ Becoming an active listener
- ◆ Evaluating your own accent

Did you know that when you were born you came fully equipped with a built-in universal language processing system? Your parents didn't even have to place a special order. It came standard in all models—and still does to this day. But although everyone's brain is capable of hearing and potentially speaking every single language on the planet, most people ignore all but one. In fact, most of us become so specialized in our mother tongue that our brains eventually shut out the sounds and rhythms of all the others.

Now that's not to say that you can't learn another language. It's obvious that you can—and did. But because you weren't surrounded with the sounds and rhythms of American English in your earliest years, your brain now has to work harder to access the information it formerly considered unnecessary. That explains why you don't pronounce—and maybe don't even hear—some of the more subtle nuances of the language. Is it possible to bridge that linguistic divide? Yes, of course it's possible, if you listen to my advice and start listening, which is what this chapter is all about.

The Standard American English Accent

I've been talking about the standard American English accent since the beginning of the book. Now it's time to get more specific about what that actually is. Rather than my trying to explain it to you, I suggest you listen to one of the many experts who talk that particular brand of talk for a living. Just turn on your TV and listen to the accent that's used by major TV news anchors and actors on serious dramas. What you'll hear is the accent that has become the standard benchmark for professional America. It's the accent that most Americans perceive as neutral because it doesn't offer any hints about where the speaker is from. Perhaps the best way to think of it is sort of a "non-accent accent." Actually it's a blend of endless varieties of American English that makes any differences unidentifiable. Some liken it to a Midwestern or a California accent. If that's the case, however, it means that people in those areas have no discernible accent because the key component of the standard American English accent is geographic anonymity.

But we need to dig deeper for a more detailed examination. Think back to your high school biology class when you were presented with a rubbery frog and a scalpel and you had to dissect the poor creature to find out what made it tick. We're going to do something similar with the American accent, fortunately without that overwhelming scent of formaldehyde.

As with all accents, the standard American English accent is a unique blend of intonation—the music or melody of the language, and pronunciation—the way the sounds of a language are produced or pronounced. But you need to know more.

American Intonation

Because intonation comprises many elements, it's difficult to get a clear picture using only written words. Once again, I refer you to the TV broadcaster. This time when you listen, try to focus less on what the broadcaster is saying and more on the techniques he or she uses to get the message across. Notice how the pitch of the person's voice rises and falls, how some words are grouped together, and how key words are emphasized or stressed. Listen to how the broadcaster pauses after some word groups, and then speeds up again. Although there are many peaks and valleys in delivery, the overall result is strong, distinctive, and smooth. What you are hearing is perfect standard American intonation. After all, a television broadcaster is a professional.

Now, change the channel to a situation comedy. Once again pay more attention to how thoughts are being expressed than to what is being said. Also pay attention to the characters and the intonation they use in different situations. This is closer to the intonation pattern of everyday American speech. American intonation is like Americans. According to Ann Cook, author of *American Accent Training* (Barron's Educational Series, 2000), we're "loud and brassy" and our intonation is similar to the music that is indigenous to our country—jazz. Our sounds are big, loud, and emphatic. If it were put to music, you'd probably call for a saxophone, trumpet, and maybe a trombone or two.

Is intonation really that important to achieving an American accent, you ask? No, it's not important. It's absolutely critical! There are two reasons why. Proper intonation helps get your message across by conveying your thoughts, and it also communicates your attitude, emotions, and moods.

> **Stumbling Block**
>
> Many non-native English speakers have strong accents because they have learned English primarily by reading. English is not a phonetic language. What you see is not what you get. Today's spellings are based on the way words were pronounced in the seventeenth century!

American Pronunciation

If intonation is the melody of American English, think of pronunciation as its notes. It's simply the way you produce, or articulate, the sounds of a language. There may be many sounds in American English that are causing you difficulty—or maybe you're having trouble with just one or two. It's likely that the sounds that are tying your tongue in knots may not even exist in your native language. Remember how we talked about your brain shutting out sounds that you weren't exposed to in your early years? Now you will need to listen closely to re-train your ear—and your brain.

A Surprising Strategy

Although many accent programs have you labor over the specific sounds of American English, the most important area you need to work on is your intonation. That may be surprising to you, but speaking with an American intonation is so important that studies have found that when you come closer to the American melody of speech, you will be far better understood. To put it another way, improving your intonation is more essential than changing the specific sounds that you make.

You will find that as your intonation improves, your listener's ability to understand you will improve as well. But it goes beyond that. Because intonation carries so much information about your meaning and attitude, you might be misunderstood or be perceived as rude or demanding if your intonation is different from that of standard American English.

Will I ignore pronunciation in this program? No way. That's important, too. But you will work on the difficulties that you are having with American English vowels and consonants in the context of proper intonation.

Retraining Your Brain

Let's compare the way you learned to speak your native tongue with the way you learned to speak English. Although there's no way you can remember the specifics of learning your first language, I can tell you for certain that you learned it like every other person on Earth. You listened to your parents and repeated what they said. You started experimenting with the sounds you heard and put those sounds together to form words. After you associated those words with some meaning, you repeated them until you were brave enough to test them out in simple phrases and sentences. As you grew, you became more familiar with the intricacies and rhythms of your language. After a while you didn't have to think very much about it; it became habit.

Now think about how you learned to speak English. Chances are, it was primarily by *looking at* individual sounds and putting them together. You may have been taught by a non-native English speaker, so it was primarily a connection from your eye to your brain that taught you to speak English. And although you may speak it well, you don't speak it the way Americans do because you never heard the way Americans speak it, or had limited exposure to it, at any rate.

> **Info-Nugget**
>
> Some linguists can tell what language a baby will speak when the baby is only about 9 months old. Although babies don't speak at that age, linguists can determine whether the baby will speak French, Chinese, or English just by listening to the sounds, rhythms, and intonations of the child's babbling.

We need to change all that. How? By retraining your brain to hear differently and by immersing yourself in the sounds of American English. You must train your ear to hear the differences between the way you are speaking and the way you want to speak. After this happens and you are able to recognize these distinctions easily, you will practice your new speech habits until they are naturally incorporated into your everyday speech.

Operation Immersion

A few years ago I participated in an English immersion program with Spanish executives in a remote location near Madrid. Each day, "Anglos" and Spaniards conversed one on one, in small groups, and in other verbal activities. The experience was completely in English. No Spanish was to be spoken at any time during this one- to two-week experience.

The Anglos came from Australia, the United Kingdom, Canada, and, of course, the United States. The challenge for the Spanish speakers was not only to comprehend English and speak it more fluently, but also to decipher the various accents and dialects of the English speakers.

The reason that I'm mentioning the experience here is because, as with the Spaniards in that program, you need to immerse yourself completely in proper intonation and pronunciation. Unlike the Spaniards, you will have to focus on only one English accent, the one considered "standard American." Yes, I know that the people around you are speaking American English all the time, but you are probably so busy trying to communicate that you may not actually be listening to how they're speaking. The first step in achieving the accent that you want is to hear it over and over so you can compare it to your own speech patterns and make appropriate adjustments.

Becoming an Active Listener

The more time you spend in the United States surrounded by American English speakers with a native accent, the more your accent will improve by simple osmosis. But that may take years and years and it may never happen to the extent that you wish. Think of Henry Kissinger, for example. He was born in Germany and came to the United States in 1938 at roughly 15 years of age. So he's been living in the United States for more than 70 years, yet his accent is as strong as ever. His older brother, Walter, is reported to speak with much less accented speech. Why is that? According to the elder Mr. Kissinger, his little brother "doesn't listen." Apparently, Walter Kissinger really wanted to modify his accent and became an active listener. Here are some of the ways he might have done it. I recommend you try them as well:

1. Listen to talk radio. National Public Radio (NPR) has some good selections. Close your eyes and listen to the melody of the language. After a few minutes, switch your brain to a more analytical mode and listen to the sounds that are being made within each word.

2. Rent audio books and DVDs. Get in the habit of enjoying stories or professional development programs as you commute to work each day.

3. Rent movies or watch TV and pay attention to the sounds of American speech and the way the tongue, teeth, and lips move. Americans don't use the front of their mouths to speak very often, so you will have to do some close detective work.

4. Because intonation conveys so much about our feelings and intentions, pay close attention to which words are being given greater emphasis and consider the attitude and feelings of the speaker.

5. Step out of your comfort zone and surround yourself with as many native-born American English–speaking people as possible. You will not reduce your accent much if you speak American English at work and revert to your native language at home.

6. When your participation isn't critical, become an observer in conversations. Listen and watch how people interact with each other. Don't listen as much for content, but listen to how words and phrases are being said.

7. Listen to *Voice of America*. They broadcast slower-paced English programs in their "Learning English" segment. It's a great place for active listening at www.voanews.com.

Evaluating Your Own Accent

Now you're ready for the next step. No, don't abandon your active listening skills. Continue to do what you have been doing—analyzing and appreciating good American English speech models. But now it's time to get up close and personal. In other words, it's time to listen to yourself.

The only way you can get a real handle on how strong your accent is and how much work you have to do is through self-assessment. What you will learn from this critical look at your speech will form the groundwork for a plan to achieve a more Americanized version of the way you speak.

Recording a Speech Sample

In Appendix B, you will find a written speech sample that was specifically designed by linguists to contain all the phonemes, or sounds, of the English language.

Although this self-assessment is not a perfect analysis of your speech patterns and intonation, it will give you an idea of how close your speech patterns are to the American style. It's not a substitute for a one-on-one analysis by a speech and language professional, of course, but it will provide general direction and guidance. If you would prefer a more accurate evaluation by a professional, see our Resources section in Appendix D.

> **Stumbling Block**
>
> If you don't keep your motivational level high, you will never reach your goal. The best way to stay committed is to monitor your progress. Make a speech recording every two to three weeks and listen to how different you sound each time.

What I suggest is that you make a few copies of the speech sample page (Appendix B) so you can make notes or circle areas that are giving you trouble. Date each copy. Then compare each copy with the notes about your next recording.

By the way, you don't need to go into debt to purchase a high-powered recording device. Any inexpensive tape recorder will do the trick, or there are recording programs available free on the Internet. Your own computer many contain one that will work. Look under Accessories for a sound recorder.

Track 1: Appendix B has complete instructions, but briefly—you will simply read the paragraph aloud and record it. Then listen to the way I have recorded it and compare the two versions. You might want to try it a few times. Improvement can happen very quickly when you are really listening.

> **Sound Advice**
>
> If you feel that you're not a good judge of your own speech, find a native-born American English speaker who would be willing to critique your recording. By the way, having a mentor who is willing to be honest with you and provide you with constructive feedback would be invaluable in achieving your goal.

What to Listen For

As you replay your speech sample, try to focus on the words that you are making incorrectly. Some people are really good at analyzing their speech. But remember there may be sounds in American English that might not exist in your native language, and vice versa. When that occurs, your brain may not register those sounds. In other words, you may not even hear the differences between your speech and my speech. The same is true with intonation. To you, your speech may not sound monotone or choppy, so you may not be your own best judge. You need someone more objective. That's why I recommend asking someone else for an opinion. Make sure that person is a native-born American English speaker and that he or she won't have any difficulty offering an honest evaluation of your speech. If you're thinking about asking someone who may worry about hurting your feelings, go on to the next candidate. You need total honesty.

These are the specific issues for which you need to listen:

1. Are you adding extra sounds that shouldn't be there?

2. Are you leaving out sounds, particularly at the ends of words?

3. Are you substituting one sound for another?

4. Are you producing any sounds that don't sound quite like the model?

5. Did you stress or emphasize the same words that were stressed or emphasized in the recorded sample?

6. Was your voice monotone or choppy?

Need Some Direction?

If you are having some difficulty determining which sounds you need to target, there is a guide that lists common speech habits according to your own nationality in Appendix C. Of course, the material in the appendix is not all-inclusive, and you might not have problems with some of the sounds listed, but it's a good place to start. Take a close look at your speech sample and at Appendix C, and use this program to target the sound and intonation errors that you discover. I'll provide you with more direction as we move along.

The Least You Need to Know

- ◆ The two key components of any accent are intonation and pronunciation.

- ◆ A standard American English accent conveys no hints about where the speaker is from.

- ◆ Producing a standard American English intonation will help modify your accent more than working on individual sound difficulties.

- ◆ Immerse yourself in the sounds of American English, become an active listener, and improve your accent.

- ◆ Recording a speech sample on a regular basis will help you evaluate your progress and motivate you to continue.

Chapter

3

Setting Yourself Up for Success

In This Chapter

♦ Developing your plan of action

♦ Learning why "speech triggers" are essential

♦ Discovering why it's important to take risks

♦ Considering an entirely new alphabet

Some people are intimidated by the idea of accent reduction. Obviously you're not one of them or you wouldn't be here. But many people I've spoken to are under the impression that modifying their accent means having to learn to speak in an entirely new way. That's not the case at all. When you reduce an accent you are actually gaining an awareness of the way you currently speak and acquiring new habits that are closer to the American rhythm and sound system. So rather than speaking in a new way, you'll be modifying the way you already speak. But it doesn't happen overnight. It takes tenacity, commitment, and personal planning. And it takes a strategy to move that plan forward.

Your Plan of Action

Your plan starts with improving your intonational skills. I've already talked about why that is so important. In fact, it's the number one factor that is standing in the way of your sounding more American. Compared to the American style, your speech may sound monotone, choppy, or nasal. If you want to reduce your accent, let's deal with *intonation* first.

def•i•ni•tion

Intonation is the music or rhythm of a language. Think of pronunciation as the notes.

Next we'll target those pesky sound errors. After you have identified the specific sounds that are difficult for you to pronounce, you'll practice them in words, in phrases, and then in sentences. Sentence practice will provide a great opportunity to work on sound errors and intonation at the same time.

The Steps to Reach Your Goals

Regardless of how heavy your accent is and no matter how many sounds you need to work on, your strategy will be the same. It's accomplished in three steps:

Step 1: Hear it. To change your non-native accent, you need to hear the differences between the way you speak and the way you want to speak. Being an active listener is something we've already discussed and, hopefully, it's something you're already doing. To stress how important it is, let me put it this way: Your non-native accent will improve in direct proportion to the level of awareness you have achieved by listening.

Step 2: Feel it. After you've listened to the American intonation for a while, you'll begin to feel its unique rhythms. When you do, you'll find that you will adjust to the American style quite easily. The same is true for pronunciation, but in a different way. After you have identified the sounds you want to correct, you need to physically feel how the sound is produced before you incorporate those changes into your everyday speech.

Step 3: Practice it. When you start to become familiar with American intonation—and after you have identified sound errors and learned how to correct them—there is only one way that your new skills will become part of your everyday speech … practice.

Sound Advice

When faced with a situation in which someone has trouble understanding you, speak more slowly and look directly at the person. If you're on the phone, speak at a normal conversational level. Try to re-word what you are saying if the listener is unable to understand your message.

How Do You Get to Carnegie Hall?

There's an old American joke about one man who stops another on the streets of New York City and asks, "How do you get to Carnegie Hall?" The answer he is given is "Practice. Practice. Practice." Depending on how long you've lived in this country and your familiarity with New York City, you may or may not know that Carnegie Hall is a famous concert venue that has been around since 1891. But regardless of whether you see the humor in the joke, you need to pay attention to the punch line. How will you reduce your non-native American accent? Practice. Practice. Practice.

Of course, that's not surprising to you, is it? The only way you can incorporate a newly learned behavior into your speech is to use it so often that you don't need to think about it. But finding time to do that within your already busy schedule might not be as easy as you think. Yes, I know you have the best of intentions and will pledge to practice as much as you can throughout each day. But sometimes your daily routine and other obligations get in your way and before you know it, the day is over and you forgot to practice.

Speech Triggers

One of the best ways of reminding yourself to use new sounds and intonation patterns is by using speech triggers. In her book *Accent Reduction 101*, Elizabeth Peterson, a noted speech and language pathologist and accent reduction specialist, talks about how using speech triggers can help you remember to practice throughout the day. Later in this chapter, we talk about some strategies you can use when you're alone, but speech triggers are ways for you to practice in the real world.

So what is a speech trigger? It's something that occurs in your daily routine that will prompt you to use your newly learned speech patterns. When these events occur, they will cause the proverbial light bulb to flash over your head and serve as a trigger, or reminder, that you need to use your new skills. Because your schedule is undoubtedly a busy one, you need to think about establishing speech triggers as a priority. When you do, you will find that it's a much more effective approach to practicing your newly learned speech than putting it in your day planner or just thinking that you'll remember to practice on your own.

Stumbling Block

Fear of embarrassment is a major roadblock to success. Many people hesitate to try newly learned speech habits because they're afraid people will think they sound funny. Consider speech triggers as dress rehearsals. The more you use them, the more confident and less awkward you will feel.

A Day in the Life of Ernesto Garcia

Let's try a personal example to give you a better idea of how speech triggers work. Meet Ernesto Garcia. Ernesto is from Barcelona, Spain, and his native language is Catalan. His conversational English is very good but he has a very difficult time with one particular sound—the sound that the letter *s* stands for. In his native language, the S sound is pronounced the way Americans pronounce the letters *th*. To an American listener, it sounds as if Ernesto has a lisp.

Ernesto has done a lot of active listening. He can hear the differences between his intonation and the American style, and he is working on bringing them closer together. He is also able to distinguish the difference between the S and TH sounds. He is aware of how he produces the sound and the way the sound *should* be produced. He practices at home using the correct version when he thinks about it, but Ernesto has a busy life and he often forgets. He knows that he needs to use the corrected sound consistently in his conversation for at least three weeks for it to become habitual, but he's having difficulty finding time to practice on a regular basis. To solve the problem, Ernesto has developed a series of speech triggers to help him practice and reach his goal.

Ernesto walks into his office every morning and encounters his first speech trigger. It's the coffee maker. As with any office, near the coffee maker is the place where everyone gathers to make small talk, compare their weekends, discuss what was on TV the previous night, and talk about the day ahead. As he talks to his colleagues, using his correct sound is uppermost in Ernesto's mind, and he uses this time to incorporate his newly learned skills in these casual conversations.

There are other speech triggers that Ernesto uses when he gets to his desk. As an added reminder, he has placed a list of key business-related phrases that he often uses on the desk near the telephone. He has underlined the *s* in each word as an additional reminder to produce the correct sound. When the phone rings (speech trigger #2), the sound prompts Ernesto to incorporate the correct sound in his telephone greeting and throughout the conversation. When it's time for lunch, the company cafeteria now has another purpose. It serves as speech trigger #3 and is a reminder to use corrected sounds in his lunchtime conversations with his colleagues.

On the way home, Ernesto takes advantage of a car pool that he has joined to save money and practices his new speech habits. That's speech trigger #4, if you're keeping count. By the way, Ernesto has informed the other car riders what he's trying to do and they gently correct him when he makes a mistake.

> **Sound Advice**
>
> Make a commitment about changing your non-native accent, and put it in writing. Then tell people what you've done. This "public accountability" will motivate you and help keep you on track.

Do you see how speech triggers work? We don't want to get too intrusive and follow Ernesto home—after all, the man does deserve some privacy. But if we were to peek in the window, we would discover that Ernesto uses speech triggers there as well. Perhaps dinner conversation with the family is another speech trigger, or speaking with his wife alone after dinner. It doesn't matter what the speech triggers are, just that they occur on a regular basis throughout the day and prompt you to speak with the new skills that you have learned.

Although I'm certain that you could come up with your own list of speech triggers, here are some examples to get the thought process started.

Speech triggers at work:

♦ Conducting a meeting

♦ Having lunch with a co-worker

♦ Answering the telephone

♦ Meeting with your boss

Speech triggers in your community:

♦ Ordering at restaurants

♦ Asking for help in a store

♦ Making a banking transaction

♦ Picking up a prescription

Speech triggers at home:

♦ Conversing during dinner

♦ Speaking to a neighbor or friend

♦ Playing a game with the family

♦ Greeting people

Creating a Speech Notebook

There's a parallel technique that you can use along with your speech triggers strategy. It's another recommendation from *Accent Reduction 101*. In her work with numerous clients, Ms. Peterson found that those who used a "speech notebook" demonstrated faster progress than those who didn't. It's a simple technique, and although it does take some discipline and commitment, it's definitely worth the effort if you can see results faster.

The notebook can be used for many purposes, but one idea is to write down three things that you know you're going to say that day. You might choose a telephone greeting or some business jargon, perhaps. Keep your statements simple. Highlight the words you know will give you difficulty and underline words that you'll need to stress. (We'll learn more about stress in Chapter 4.) Practice the sentences a few times before your day begins, and when the time comes to deliver the sentences, you'll be ready with the proper delivery.

A speech notebook is also an ideal place to keep a list of vocabulary words that you're not sure how to pronounce. Ask a native speaker about the proper way to pronounce the words, and record them so you can refer to the recording in case you forget. After you have created a list of 5 to 10 words, create sentences for each of those words and use them for practice.

Just as our friend Ernesto did, you can reserve a page in your speech notebook to write out statements that you typically say at work. Drill work or repetition are important parts of integrating corrected speech into everyday conversation, but using corrected speech in phrases that you actually say will have more meaning and impact.

Top Ten Practice Tips

If you're a fan of David Letterman, you probably look forward to the part of his show where he recites his "Top 10" list on the topic of the day. Although the list you're about to read lacks Dave's famous wit and drum roll, it does contain some valuable suggestions. Give them a try!

1. Observe the mouth movements of native speakers and do your best to imitate them. This also holds true when you're watching TV. Observe what the actors are doing with their tongue, teeth, and lips. (It's much easier now with HDTV.) If a certain word you hear sounds a bit strange, it could be because you are not pronouncing it correctly.

2. Become more aware of the intonation, or melody, of American English. We'll deal with this in much greater detail in our next chapter, but whenever you practice active listening, remember that it's not just about letter-sound differences. Listen to the melody of what people are saying as well.

3. Until you feel you have a better understanding of American English intonation and rhythm, slow down a little. If you speak too quickly and have the wrong intonation, native speakers will have a difficult time understanding you.

4. Make your dictionary your best friend. Not only will it help you with definitions, it will help you with pronunciation. In Chapter 6 you will learn about phonetic symbols. Though I have organized this program so it's not essential for you to learn them, phonetic symbols give you an advantage. When you come across an unfamiliar word, you can look up its exact pronunciation without asking anyone else for help.

5. Make a list of words that you use frequently and that are difficult for you to pronounce. Then ask a native speaker to pronounce them for you. Practice them over and over and use them in sentences. Record them so you can hear your progress.

6. Because word endings can be troublesome, pay close attention to the end of each word, paying special attention to the *s* and *ed* endings.

7. Take 15 to 20 minutes every day and read aloud. This will help you strengthen the mouth muscles that you need for speaking new sounds.

8. Record your own voice and listen for pronunciation errors. Date your recording sessions to keep track of progress. Here's a quick way to test yourself with a certain sound or phrase: leave yourself a voice-mail message.

9. Ask for help. If you have children, grandchildren, or close colleagues who are native-born American English speakers, enlist their support. Tell them that you want to be corrected. Many people feel that they will be hurting your feelings when they point out sound and intonation errors. So tell them that you welcome their input.

10. Be patient with yourself. Changing your accent is not going to happen overnight. Give yourself permission to make mistakes and just keep at it. With this book and your commitment to change, it will happen.

Take Some Risks

The eleventh tip I have for you is this: take risks! What's risky about learning and practicing new sounds, you ask? Nothing if you're in your bedroom, but what if you're speaking to your new boss or someone you've just met? Using new sound patterns in these situations can be risky, even embarrassing, if you make a mistake.

Frankly, when you first introduce new sound patterns into your speech, they will sound funny, but more to you than to anyone else. After all, you've been speaking in your current style for a number of years. What you are now trying to accomplish is to exchange one habit for another. It's bound to sound strange and awkward at first.

Before trying out new skills, first practice in comfortable and safe sur-roundings. Continue to focus on your speech triggers and think of them as dress rehearsals to build up courage. Practice new speech hab-its in conversations with your family and those you feel close to. Then take a risk—and then another. The more risks you take, the faster you will see results, and the stronger your confidence will become.

The International Phonetic Alphabet

I have one final piece of advice before I send you on the road to success. It's optional, but it's something I'd like you to consider—learning the International Phonetic Alphabet (IPA). "Just what I need," you're think-ing, "I'm having enough trouble with the 26 letters I already know about." Well, this alphabet is different. It's a phonetic alphabet and has nothing to do with letters. Rather, it has to do with the sounds of a par-ticular language.

The IPA is considered by linguists to be one of the most important achievements over the past century because anyone can learn it and use it to represent the sounds of any language. It's a systematic way of transcribing virtually every human sound on the planet. Each symbol represents one particular sound. It gives linguists a common code with which they can talk about the sounds of the world's languages. And it gives you a way to pronounce any word in any language without asking someone for assistance.

I'm mentioning this to you because you may have studied other accent reduction programs and may already be familiar with the IPA. But if you are a "first-timer" trying to decipher the different symbols and sounds, it may seem a bit overwhelming. With that thought in mind, in the upcoming sections that have to do with consonant and vowel pronunciation, I have "spelled" each sound using the English alphabet, but have also included phonetic symbols where appropriate.

I'd like you to keep an open mind and think about learning the IPA. It can be an invaluable resource now and in the future. Whenever you open a dictionary, you will not only be able to find how the word is spelled, but you can also find exactly how that word is pronounced if you are familiar with the IPA. There are several excellent resources related to the IPA in Appendix D.

The Least You Need to Know

◆ Your primary goal is to use a standard American English intonation.

◆ You will work on sound errors within the context of the principles of intonation.

◆ Using speech triggers will be a more effective reminder than just a generalized commitment to do better.

◆ A speech notebook will result in greater results, faster.

◆ Learning the International Phonetic Alphabet can be helpful in learning how to pronounce any word on your own.

Part 2

Capturing the Melody of American English

Have you ever thought of a language as having its own distinct melody? Every language does, you know. But after we become intimately familiar with our own language, we take it for granted and fail to appreciate what makes it truly unique.

In Part 2, we begin to dissect the American accent by concentrating on what makes American English distinctive—and that's primarily its intonational qualities.

Words alone can't make conversations interesting. You need to string them together like notes in a melody, change their pitch occasionally to create emphasis, and combine words into thought groups, stressing the ones that are most important to you. Not only does this help make your speech more intelligible, you'll find that listeners will hang on your every word.

We also focus on the difficulties you may be having with some American sounds. As you will discover, however, intonation is much more important. With proper American intonation, you will find communication to be much easier.

Join me for an intonation "makeover." You'll be amazed at the confidence you'll gain as you adapt to the American intonational style.

Chapter 4

Your Intonation Makeover

In This Chapter

- The importance of the syllable
- Discovering the benefits of stress
- Stressing content and function words

I have a confession to make. I'm intrigued by makeover shows. Apparently much of America is, too, because the shows seem to be all over the place. Sometimes it's not an entire show, but what they call an "ambush makeover." Some unsuspecting subject will be grabbed by a producer while standing outside the *Today Show*, for example. Sixty minutes later, out she comes with a new hairstyle and lip-gloss and everyone gasps!

What does that have to do with accent reduction, you're asking? Actually, it's right on the mark because you—yes, lucky *you!*—have been chosen for a major makeover in the intonation department! Yes, it will take longer than 60 minutes, but with time and practice, this transformation will last a lifetime!

The Amazing Transformation!

In case you're not as familiar with makeovers as I am, you need to know that there's always a before shot prior to "the big reveal." That's TV talk for the moment the finished product is unveiled. What I'd like you to do is to think of this concept in terms of your intonation.

Before your intonation makeover:

You are speaking with the rhythm and melody of your native language. If you are Middle Eastern or Asian, you may sound choppy or monotone by American standards. If you are a native Spanish speaker, you may have a rise in pitch on vowel sounds. If you are a native speaker from the Caribbean, you have a lilting or sing-song intonation pattern affecting your speech. Of course, it's impossible to discuss the characteristics and intonation pattern of every culture and every country—but every language has a unique intonational rhythm. And so does American English.

After your intonation makeover:

What a transformation! It's as if I'm listening to an entirely different person! Just listen to yourself!

♦ Your speech is much more intelligible. Finally, people aren't asking you to repeat yourself.

♦ Your speech is no longer flat or mechanical. The patterns of your native tongue are much less obvious.

♦ Your speech is more fluid. You are speaking in a pleasing manner that truly engages your listener.

♦ You are finding that the sound errors you make are less noticeable. Yes, you're still making some mistakes, but somehow they don't seem to be getting in the way of people understanding you.

♦ You sound stronger, persuasive, and dynamic, and you feel more confident.

How did that transformation occur? Did someone wave a magic wand? No, you did it all yourself—by turning yourself into a human sponge. You soaked up all there was to know about the American intonational patterns. And not only did you learn about it, you listened to it. Your awareness increased to the point that you were easily able to distinguish your melody of speech from the American style, and you learned how to adapt from one to the other.

What exactly did you hear? You heard the peaks and valleys, the changes in pitch, the pauses and the word groupings. And you learned the critical role that stress plays in American intonation. That's probably the single most important thing you learned. Now for the big question: are you ready to undergo that makeover for real?

Syllable Countdown and Stress

Your intonation makeover starts by analyzing intonation from the ground up. It begins with the sound patterns of individual words and expands from there. When you listen to any word, you can hear its individual components or syllables.

There's an important feature about American English that is critical to your producing an American intonational pattern of speech. It's essential that you realize that English is a *stress-timed language.* Americans place emphasis on certain syllables and also on particular words within sentences. This may be completely different from your native language. In some languages, maybe yours, equal weight is given to each syllable or sound unit. Not in English.

def•i•ni•tion

> Rather than give equal importance to all syllables and words, a **stress-timed language** emphasizes certain syllables within words and certain words within sentences.

Let me give you an example using the common word *baseball.* How many syllables does it have? You can hear it, can't you? Base-ball. Yes, two syllables. But now we need to know which syllable is stressed. Say the word out loud and see if you can hear which syllable has more emphasis. It's the first syllable—BASE-ball.

Let's try another. What about the word *intonation?* Think about it. Then say it. In-to-na-tion. Right! Four syllables. Which one is stressed? In-to-NA-tion. The third syllable. When you say it out loud, you'll hear that you're treating that syllable differently than the others. You're giving it additional emphasis, or stress, by changing your pitch or stretching it out a little longer.

Why Bother?

Is it essential that you be able to count syllables to change your accent? The answer is "no" and "yes." No one is going to ask you how many syllables are contained in the words you say, but there are reasons that it's important. Here are the reasons:

1. If you stress a word incorrectly, it can be difficult to understand, and you might convey a different thought entirely. So as your vocabulary increases and you learn new words, it's important to learn how a word is stressed at the same time you learn its meaning. Here's an example. Think of the word *contest*. If you put the accent on the first syllable—CON-test—it's a noun meaning a competition of some sort. Put the accent on the second syllable and you have con-TEST, a verb meaning to dispute an issue.

2. Paying close attention to syllables will assist you in fine-tuning your listening skills.

3. Counting syllables and determining which syllable is stressed will help you pay more attention to the entire word and will prevent you from eliminating parts of words that should be pronounced.

4. Syllables will help segment your speech and contribute to its rhythm, giving it stronger and weaker beats. Syllables are the first step in creating an interesting speech melody. Plus, on a more practical level, they make speech easier to pronounce and process.

Sound Advice

Regardless of what the word is and how many syllables it has, only one syllable in each word is stressed, or given additional emphasis.

Test Yourself

Let's try a few. Remember first to say the word out loud and to feel the natural syllable breaks in each word. Then say the word again and feel which syllable is demanding more attention. Your voice rises a bit, your pitch is higher, and you are giving more importance to that syllable.

 Track 2: Listen as I say the words on the list. Then determine the number of syllables in each word and which syllable is stressed.

student	senate
Constitution	Obama
president	independence

The Secret of the Schwa

Are you familiar with the schwa? Although you might not have heard the word itself, you certainly have heard the sound. The schwa, in fact, is the most frequently occurring sound in spoken English, but many speakers—even native-born American English speakers—may not be technically familiar with it. But the schwa is important. In fact, it's beyond important. Learning to use the schwa is critical in helping you to improve your accent.

As you already know, syllables are not all created equal. In the words you've just analyzed, you learned that some syllables are given more weight than others. Some syllables are stressed and others are unstressed or reduced. When you stress a particular syllable, its vowel is pronounced in a long clear manner. What about the vowel in an unstressed or reduced syllable? It's replaced by what we call the schwa, a low pitched "uh" sound. You may see it sometimes on a chart represented by an upside-down and backward *e*. It looks like this: ə.

> **Info-Nugget**
>
> Of all the vowel sounds in English, the schwa is the most common. Oddly, it has no written symbol in the English alphabet. It can be represented by any vowel.

Let me give you an example. When you said *student* in our syllable countdown list, you realized it had two syllables and the accent was on the first—STU-dent. But what about that second syllable? You didn't say stu-dent, giving equal importance to each syllable. You said STU-dent, and the *e* in the unstressed syllable sounded like "uh," so the word actually was pronounced STU-duhnt.

What you need to remember is that to be understood and have proper American intonation, vowels in stressed syllables are pronounced with a somewhat higher pitch and vowel sounds in a reduced syllable are usually replaced by the schwa sound. This is an essential component of the American rhythm of speech.

The Schwa in Disguise

I will admit that this concept is somewhat complicated, so we'll continue with a little more practice until you feel more comfortable. Let's take a closer look at some words that contain the schwa.

As we said, the schwa sound takes the place of the vowel sound in any reduced syllable. That means that any vowel can represent the schwa sound—*a*, *e*, *i*, *o*, *u*, and sometimes *y*. This is one of the reasons that spelling in English is so difficult. It is hard to know what letter the schwa sound represents.

Stumbling Block

English pronunciation does not always match the spelling. If you have learned English from seeing the words in print, it is very important for you to stop thinking about words the way they are written. English spelling comes from many different places. It is not consistent.

Beginning English-speakers often make the mistake of pronouncing every vowel in its strong, pure form. But it's perfectly acceptable—in fact, it's the American standard—to use the schwa in an unstressed syllable. Although it may sound odd or sloppy to you at first, Americans don't consider it that way. Even the most articulate broadcaster uses the schwa. Until you can learn the proper use of the schwa, your spoken American English rhythm will sound accented.

Schwa Practice

Track 3: Let's analyze some words. Each has a different syllable count, and each has a different vowel that represents the schwa.

1. **ad<u>e</u>pt**—The *a* represents the schwa in *adept.* The word has two syllables and the accent is on the second syllable. The *a* in the unaccented syllable is pronounced "uh."

2. **synth<u>e</u>sis**—The *e* represents the schwa in *synthesis.* The word has three syllables and the accent is on the first syllable. The *e* in the unaccented syllable is pronounced "uh."

3. **dec<u>i</u>mal**—The *i* represents the schwa in *decimal.* The word has three syllables and the accent is on the first syllable. The *i* in the unaccented syllable is pronounced "uh."

4. **harm<u>o</u>ny**—The *o* represents the schwa in *harmony.* The word has three syllables and the accent is on the first syllable. The *o* in the unaccented syllable is pronounced "uh."

5. **medi<u>u</u>m**—The *u* represents the schwa in *medium.* The word has three syllables and the accent is on the first syllable. The *u* in the unaccented syllable is pronounced "uh."

6. **s<u>y</u>ringe**—The *y* represents the schwa in *syringe.* The word has two syllables and the accent is on the second syllable. The unaccented *y* is pronounced "uh."

Sentence Stress

Just as words have stressed and unstressed syllables, sentences contain regular patterns of stressed and unstressed words. You've already learned that syllables do not get equal treatment. Words are also not created equal. In English, we stress specific words and quickly glide over the less meaningful ones. To some non-native speakers, it's hard to understand why we stress some words and appear to almost swallow others.

Words, Not Created Equal

Track 4: There is an exercise that many teachers of English as a second language use to demonstrate the importance of stress in American English. Listen to the exercise.

Now read these two sentences aloud:

1. The <u>beautiful</u> <u>mountain</u> <u>appeared</u> <u>transfixed</u> in the <u>distance</u>.

2. <u>He</u> can <u>come</u> on <u>Sundays</u> as long as he doesn't have to do any <u>homework</u> in the <u>evening</u>.

If we were to time the first sentence, it would take you about five seconds to say it. The second sentence would also take about five seconds to say.

But how can that be? The first sentence is much shorter and has fewer syllables than the second one. It's because of the stressed nature of the English language. This simple exercise makes a very important point about how we speak and use the language.

Let's analyze this further. Even though the second sentence is approximately 30 percent longer than the first, the sentences take the same time to speak. This is because there are five stressed words in each sentence. From this example, you can see that you need to pay special attention to the stressed words, pronouncing them as clearly as possible. Although pronouncing every word correctly is important, correct pronunciation of stressed words will greatly improve your intelligibility to American listeners.

The next time you're watching TV or speaking with friends who are native-born English speakers, do some listening detective work. Listen to how their conversation focuses on stressed words rather than giving importance to each word. You will soon find that you can understand and communicate better because you will begin to listen for stressed words, and then you will use them in your own conversation. It's likely that you will find out that all the words you thought you didn't understand were really not crucial for understanding the general sense of the conversation or making yourself understood. You can see why stressed words are the key to better pronunciation and comprehension of American English.

Content Words and Function Words

Now that you know that American intonation emphasizes stressing specific words, the logical question is, "How do you know which words in a sentence to stress?"

Here's the rule: We stress content words and place less stress on function words.

Content words are the most meaningful words in a sentence. They're the most important elements you want to communicate. A good way to understand this is to think back to the days when people sent telegrams. Because they had to pay by the word, telegrams contained only vital information. The words people included were content words; they were absolutely essential to the message.

Let's see if I can give you a better idea of what I mean. If, for example, you were arrested for disorderly conduct far away from home and your cellmate is threatening you with bodily harm, your telegram might read something such as this: ARRESTED. NEED $500 BAIL. QUICK.

Content words convey the most important information. Here are the kinds of content words:

◆ Nouns—names of persons, places, things, and ideas

◆ Main verbs—words that convey action

◆ Adjectives—descriptive words that modify or describe nouns

◆ Adverbs—words that modify verbs

Function words are words that tie content words together. Because they don't convey essential information, speakers don't give them as much stress or importance. Here are the types of function words, plus a few examples of each:

◆ Determiners—*the, a, some, a few*

◆ Auxiliary verbs—*don't, can, were*

◆ Prepositions—*to, on, before, opposite*

◆ Conjunctions—*but, while, as*

◆ Pronouns—*I, she, he, they, us*

Sound Advice

Remember that content words are the most meaningful in a sentence and receive more stress. Words that tie the content words together are called function words and are given less vocal importance.

The Ups and Downs of Intonation

Now you know that the content words need to be stressed and the function words do not. But exactly how do you stress words? Perhaps you are an exceptionally good listener and can already tell me what the answer is. What exactly happened when you heard me stress a particular word in the speech sample and in previous tracks on the CD? What did I do to make the stressed words stand apart from the less important ones? If you heard it but just can't explain it, let's talk about a popular method of teaching intonation that some linguists use.

Although there are several popular strategies, I think the one created by Dr. David Allen Stern is the simplest and most effective. In his program, *The Sound & Style of American English* (Dialect Accent Specialists, 2006), he explains his "Jump Up & Step Down" pattern of pitch change. What that means is that inside each phrase or thought group, the pitch jumps up to a higher note on an early, important word. Then it steps down a little bit on each syllable that follows within that unit. It's a pattern that Americans use, but most speakers of English as a second language don't. In fact, speakers of some languages use little or no pitch change; others use upward glides in pitch to emphasize ideas. What do Americans do? Jump up on the most important content words, then step down. How many times do you jump up in a sentence? It depends on how long the sentence is and what you think is important.

Track 5: Listen to these examples. After you hear me say each sentence, try it yourself. Just remember to jump up in pitch on the most important word, then step down in pitch and continue to move down until you reach the next important word. Then you jump up again in pitch to give the next important word or idea the emphasis it needs. By the way, you can jump up on whatever word you wish, depending on which words you decide are important and need to stand out from the others.

Nouns

1. I had LOBSTER for lunch.

2. I think it might SNOW this afternoon.

3. ENGLISH is a difficult language to learn.

Verbs

1. The witness SAW you that night.

2. I SWEAR to tell the truth.

Adjectives

1. She is a BEAUTIFUL woman.

2. You're doing an EXCELLENT job modifying your accent.

Adverbs

1. I need you to come QUICKLY!

2. You have TOTALLY lost it!

Are you brave enough to try a sentence with more than one stressed word?

Imagine an irate person saying this:

> MARY bought BANANAS at the BODEGA when I DISTINCTLY told her to buy PEARS at the SUPERMARKET.

Revert to Your Former Language

Here's an exercise that Dr. David Alan Stern suggests. Read the following sentence group expressively, and do it with your native accent. As you are speaking, pay attention to what you're doing to stress important words. Now translate the sentence into your first language, again speaking with enthusiasm—and really pay attention to what you are doing to stress ideas.

The exercise should demonstrate to you that you already know when to stress important words. But in your native language you are using different tools for pitch and loudness to create the same effect. So now you know the difference between your old pattern and the American jump up and down style. After you adapt it, your accent will be far less obvious. Ready to give it a go? Say these sentences aloud. Stress the words that appear in capital letters.

I'm VERY pleased to meet you.

THANK you SO much for giving me a call.

I TRIED to make an appointment for NEXT week, but you were busy.

I WON'T be seeing OTHER patients until the FOLLOWING Monday.

Sound Advice _____

If you stress the wrong syllable of a word, it can be very difficult to understand. It is important to learn how a word is stressed when you learn how to pronounce it. If your native language does not have a word stress pattern like that of English, you will need to be especially conscientious when you learn the English forms.

Time to Hit Bottom

I'm sure that by now you can see how the jump up, step down strategy can add interest and melody to your speech. Plus it helps you refine your message by calling attention to the words that you feel are really important.

But what happens when you jumped up and jumped down and you are at the end of your message? It's critical that you end the sentence on a downward beat. Not doing so makes you sound as if you are not sure of yourself. When you watch a TV newscaster or listen to a powerful speaker, you will notice that after he or she has concluded a sentence full of meaningful pitch jumps, he ultimately moves the pitch down for the rest of the statement. This simple technique of ending with a much lower pitch goes a long way to making you sound more persuasive and more confident.

 Track 6: Listen to the following sentences. Notice that I end each sentence on a downward pitch.

1. The marketing director suggested we put together a focus group.

2. Proper intonation is vital to your success in reducing your accent.

3. Take three aspirin and call me in the morning.

4. Ask not what your country can do for you, but what you can do for your country.

5. It will be partly sunny today with a high of 95.

Sentence Stress and Meaning

We've already talked about the fact that each word has a syllable that gets stressed. And we said that certain words in a sentence get stressed as well. In fact, stressing a certain word can change the entire tone or meaning of what you have to say. Stressing the wrong word in a sentence could result in a complete misinterpretation of your message and your mood or meaning. The following exercise will give you a better idea of what I mean.

The Red Hat Exercise

Track 7: A popular exercise among linguists and teachers is called the Red Hat Exercise. Though the words are the same in each sentence in the exercise, the stress (or jump) is placed on a different word each time. By stressing a different word, you will see that the meaning of the sentence changes. That's how important stress is!

I didn't say you stole my red hat.

>   Implication: Someone else said it.

I **DIDN'T** say you stole my red hat.

>   Implication: I deny saying it.

I didn't **SAY** you stole my red hat.

>   Implication: Maybe I wrote it.

I didn't say **YOU** stole my red hat.

>   Implication: I said someone else stole it.

I didn't say you **STOLE** my red hat.

>   Implication: I said you borrowed it, perhaps.

I didn't say you stole **MY** red hat.

>   Implication: I said you stole someone else's.

I didn't say you stole my **RED** hat.

>   Implication: I said you stole my green hat.

I didn't say you stole my red **HAT.**

>   Implication: I said you stole my red handbag.

Choosing Words to Stress

There are some other, rather complicated rules that address other reasons to stress words in a sentence. But for every rule, there's usually an exception. For now, I think you have learned enough to move forward and improve your intonation. Experiment a little! Try to feel the music of the language and add stress when you think it's important to do so. My goal is *not* to teach you to speak like an American-sounding robot. After all, it's *your* conversation. You know what message you want to convey and what words are important to you. That means that *you* should be the one to decide, ultimately, which words to stress.

The Least You Need to Know

- ◆ The schwa sound usually takes the place of the vowel in an unstressed syllable.

- ◆ Jump up on words you want to stress; then jump down from there.

- ◆ Stressing the wrong word can convey the wrong message or mood.

- ◆ Putting stress on the wrong syllable of some words can completely change the word's meaning.

- ◆ To sound professional, end statements on a downward pitch.

- ◆ There are rules about word stress within a sentence, but ultimately it's your decision to stress the words that are most important, depending on your meaning.

5

Add Rhythm and Personality!

In This Chapter

- Learning the importance of phrasing and pitch
- How sounds, words, and sentences connect
- Determining your rate of speech
- Listening to how the pros do it

I recall the advice of a professor I had for a public speaking course in college. He consistently reinforced the idea that you had to make sure you had finished speaking before your audience had finished listening. Think about that for a minute. Accent or not, everyone needs to capture and hold the listener's attention.

You have already learned some of the techniques to do just that—ways to make your speech more melodic with syllable and word stress. But there is so much more you can contribute, such as variety, rhythm, and a large dose of your own personality.

What else can you do to keep the conversational music flowing and your listeners focused on what you have to say? That's what this chapter is all about.

Pauses and Phrases

Once again, we look to the TV broadcaster to demonstrate another valuable skill, one that will benefit you on many levels. In Chapter 2, we talked about how broadcasters stress certain syllables and key words. But now I'd like you to listen for something else—their phrasing, including those dramatic pauses between phrases. Not only do phrases and pauses vary the melody of a broadcaster's presentation, they enable him or her to assemble and deliver the message in a more organized way. It also enables the speaker to do something that's essential to life—breathe.

So how does this skill help you? Chances are, you're not interested in applying for a network TV position, but there are major lessons to learn from a broadcaster's presentation. Let me see if I can make my point with a more personal example.

Let's say you are having a conversation with someone at work. It's a difference of opinion, and you have a strong case to present. To make your case more powerful, you need to offer the information to your listener in phrases or "chunks." Group your thoughts into logical units so you can present your argument more efficiently and effectively. Then deliver these ideas to your listener in sequence, separating these "thought groups" with pauses or small breaks.

What's the benefit of these pauses? The pauses give you a few seconds to think about what you've just said, enabling you to make some adjustments to upcoming thought groups—plus, the pauses give you time to take a gulp or two of air. Because your thought groups will be of varying length, with different syllables and words that are stressed, your message will have variety and rhythm. In addition, speaking this way offers the impression of strong continuity, even though there are brief starts and stops in your presentation.

From the listener's perspective, these phrases and pauses are just as vital. When you deliver your argument or message in this manner, it is easier for listeners to process your words. It gives them time to catch up with you and think about the last burst of information you delivered. It doesn't matter if you are talking to one person or to a large group, the listener becomes more engaged and comfortable listening to you when you use thought groups and pauses.

Sound Advice _____

To make it easier on both you and the listener, present your material in "chunks," or thought groups. It will make your delivery more effective, and your listener will be able to process your message more easily.

A Lesson from a Former President

Track 8: Thought groups are nothing new. Everyday speakers and prominent orators have been using them for centuries. Let's listen to an excerpt from the First Inaugural Address of Franklin Delano Roosevelt. Roosevelt was the thirty-second president, and served from 1933 to 1945. I suggest that you play this several times. The first time, follow the text as you listen. Then close your eyes and just listen. Pay close attention to President Roosevelt's overall intonation—but most especially, the thought groups.

President Hoover, Mr. Chief Justice, my friends:

This is a day of national consecration. And I am certain that on this day my fellow Americans expect that on my induction into the Presidency, I will address them with a candor and a decision which the present situation of our people impels.

This is preeminently the time to speak the truth, the whole truth, frankly and boldly. Nor need we shrink from honestly facing conditions in our country today. This great Nation will endure, as it has endured, will revive and will prosper.

So, first of all, let me assert my firm belief that the only thing we have to fear is fear itself—nameless, unreasoning, unjustified terror which paralyzes needed efforts to convert retreat into advance.

Pitch Cues

When a professional speaker comes to the end of a complete thought, his or her pitch drops. You have already learned that ending on a downbeat is the signal that a thought is finished. But what if the speaker is not finished and has more to say? If a speaker is presenting a list of items, for example, she will pause between each item, but her pitch won't drop to the lowest level. Her pitch signals that there is more to follow. If a speaker presents a thought group and ends on a higher pitch or lengthens a final syllable in that word group, you know there is more to come.

American listeners are subconsciously programmed to listen for thought groups and pauses within a conversation. They listen for pitch cues, too, because it helps to know where a speaker is, and where she might be going. Those pauses and pitch changes send a message to the listener's brain either to keep listening or that the message is complete.

Stumbling Block

Misinterpreting pitch cues can happen easily because many languages use pitch differently than does American English. To avoid misunderstanding, be certain you are familiar with the American English use of pitch.

Sound complicated? Not really. You probably use this technique all the time and simply aren't aware of it. Maybe this real-life situation in which pitch cues give direction will help.

Let's say that you are in a restaurant and you haven't quite decided what you want. The waiter asks for your order, and you're still making up your mind. However, you don't want to send him or her away! So you say, "I'll have prime rib—rare—with a baked potato and sour cream—house salad—with ranch dressing—and cheesecake for dessert."

Pretend you're in that situation and act out that sentence. Don't read it, act it. As you do, listen to your pitch when you come to each dash. The pitch goes up slightly each time and conveys a message to the waiter that there is more information to follow; the waiter knows to keep listening. When you got to the final phrase—"and cheesecake for dessert"—your pitch dropped to its lowest level. That told the waiter you were finished ordering.

It's very important that you understand and can appreciate the American pattern of phrasing and pauses. It may be very different from that of your native language, but it will cause misunderstanding if not done correctly. For example, some East Indian languages use pitch falls to indicate that the speaker is about to make the most important point. To an English listener, that could be confusing because he will interpret the drop to be the end of the remark and perhaps even the end of the conversation.

The Right Connections

There is yet another element that's essential to modifying a non-native accent: word connections, or liaisons. It's something that I'm certain you've noticed as an active listener. As you know, Americans don't speak one word at a time. Rather, they speak in logically connected groups of words. The key to gaining a natural, smooth-flowing style of speech is to connect those words within groups. Most of the time the end of one word attaches to the beginning of the next word.

If someone or something were to land here from another planet and hear Americans conversing, that alien would think that English is made up of one giant word. Yes, of course, there are the pauses that we talked about earlier for breath and comprehension—but so much of our speech is linked from one word to the next. Is this a random thing? No, believe it or not, there is a method to this seeming madness.

There are three primary ways that words are linked in American English, but before I discuss them with you, I want to offer some advice. Read the rules and understand them—but don't dwell on them too much. Why is that? Because over-analyzing your speech will not give you the smooth intonation that you're looking for.

Stumbling Block

Speaking faster will not make your accent or sound difficulties less obvious. In fact, speaking faster will call additional attention to any errors that you're making and will make your overall speech less intelligible.

My suggestion is to get a basic understanding of what connects to what. Then keep listening to how native-born Americans do it and gradually incorporate these connections into your speech. It will feel natural after a while. These rules have come into being because they explain what American English speakers do naturally. We combine words and let one flow into the next because it requires less energy and fewer mouth movements.

Track 9: Now for the rules about how American English-speakers connect words. Remember what I said: we're just doing what comes naturally. Listen carefully.

1. **Vowel to vowel.** When one word ends in a vowel sound and the next word starts with a vowel sound, link the words.

   Why are you always so angry?

   My only apple is very yellow.

2. **Same consonant to consonant.** Link words when one word ends in a consonant sound and the next word starts with the same consonant sound.

   Give Valerie some money.

   Chet told us about his bad day.

3. **Consonant to vowel.** When a word ends in a consonant sound and the next word starts with a vowel sound, the consonant links to the vowel.

   I jumped in the pool on a hot day.

   Yes, I'd like a glass of red wine.

A Special English Lesson

One of the most valuable resources that I have come across while researching this book is *Voice of America* (*VOA*) *Special English*. Usually I would list an important resource in the back of the book, but this one is so valuable to you as you reduce your accent that it deserves more than just a listing.

VOA Special English delivers today's news and feature stories, but the broadcasters have slowed down the delivery of the material so it is easier for you to understand. The rate of speech, although slower than you might naturally speak, is still an extraordinary model for American intonation and pronunciation.

I encourage you to check it out (go to www.voanews.com/ specialenglish) and discover all the services it offers at no cost. I have included one of their broadcasts on the CD. It's an exceptional opportunity for you to take all the techniques that I have presented to this point and actually hear them put into practice by professional broadcasters.

Sound Advice

The rules for connecting one word to the other are based on what American English speakers actually do. Although you should learn the rules, you will adapt the technique faster by just listening to native-born American speech models.

What to Listen For

While you listen to the excerpt on the CD, I want you to listen not only to what the speakers are saying but how they are saying it. I suggest listening a number of times to identify the specific techniques that we have discussed throughout this book.

1. Listen for the thought groups and the pauses in between them.

2. Be aware of the pitch changes throughout.

3. Hear which syllables and individual words are stressed.

4. Pay attention to the dramatic inflections caused by stress and pitch changes.

5. Listen to how the important information ends with a downbeat.

6. Hear how words are connected to one another.

7. Listen for how the announcer uses pitch as a cue either that there is more to come or that a thought is complete.

VOA Broadcast Script

Track 10: Welcome to THIS IS AMERICA in VOA Special English. I'm Barbara Klein.

And I'm Steve Ember. This week on our program, we tell about pets in the United States.

Earlier this month, the Westminster Kennel Club held its yearly dog show in New York City. Westminster has been awarding prizes to special show dogs for 133 years. Dogs are judged against a description of the perfect dog for each kind or breed. Then one is chosen as "Best in Show." This year, more than 2,000 dogs of 170 breeds competed. The winner was a Sussex Spaniel named Stump. Stump is 10 years old—the oldest dog ever to win the championship at Westminster.

The Westminster Kennel Club was the first member of the pure breed dog registry group, The American Kennel Club. The AKC recognizes dog breeds in the United States. Every year it develops a list of the most popular breeds. The same breed has won that honor for the past 18 years—the Labrador Retriever. The club's website describes Labs as gentle, intelligent, and family friendly. Yet not all Labs are the same.

Your Rate of Speech

Your rate of speech is something that greatly impacts your intelligibility and your accent. There are many tricks that non-native English speakers use to make their accents less noticeable. One of them is to speak faster, hoping that they'll jump over the sounds they don't produce correctly. Of course, it's not an effective strategy and simply increases the chance for miscommunication. Often, in an attempt to speak faster, some consonants are dropped at the ends of words, again making their speech even more difficult to understand, further accentuating mistakes.

Your rate of speech is a huge factor in the intonation game. How fast you speak not only has to be comfortable for you, but also pleasing enough to listeners that they can understand and appreciate what you have to say.

There are a variety of factors that can influence how fast someone speaks, including how familiar the speaker is with the material, the speaker's age, and even his or her emotional state.

Info-Nugget

The average speech rate in the mid-Atlantic states is 120–140 words per minute. It's fastest in New York City. What really matters, of course, is not how many words a speaker can get out, but how many words the listener understands.

Test Your Rate of Speech

Someone has taken the trouble to develop a formula that determines how fast you speak. The formula is this:

$$\frac{(\text{the number of words spoken}) \times 60}{(\text{the number of seconds it took to speak the words})}$$

In other words, multiply the number of words spoken by 60. Then divide that product by the number of seconds it took to speak the words. The answer is the number of words spoken per minute.

So if you are really interested in knowing, you can practice reading any short passage and time yourself. Then you can calculate your rate according to the formula. The speech rates in different countries vary. The American standard seems to be recordings of books-on-tape. When actors read them, their goal is between 150–160 words per minute, which is the range in which people comfortably hear and vocalize words.

Ways to Modify Your Rate of Speech

There are some ways you can modify the results of your speech rate test:

◆ Pay attention to exactly how you are speaking. As you say each word, feel your tongue touching your teeth or feel your lips as they open and close.

◆ Match your rate of speech with another speaker. Listen to speakers you admire. Note the different rates of speech they use during the course of their conversations.

- To slow down, remember to pause, especially between phrases and sentences. Breathe, and let your listener breathe.

- Highlight the key words of your message by prolonging them slightly and raising your pitch.

- Ask for help from a native-born English speaker. If you have a speech to give, practice it in front of your mentor and ask for help. Or simply ask for a critique of your everyday speech.

- Timing yourself really does work. If you don't have a stopwatch, there are a number of online versions that work well. Here's one of them: http://stopwatch.onlineclock.net.

American Voice Quality

When I mention American voice quality, I'm referring not only to how your voice sounds, but where it comes from physically. No matter what your language or dialect, speakers form words with different styles of muscle movements. Each of these muscle movements creates a slightly different kind of voice resonance or sound quality. Some languages come from the nose, some from the throat, and some from the chest. Though Americans themselves might be overworked and overstressed, for the most part you would never know it from their speech. American English is spoken with very little muscle tension. There's very little muscle work in the lips and the front of the mouth, especially.

American English is quite the opposite of Asian, Spanish, and other European languages, which require much tighter musculature in the back of the throat. Because that tension is *not* present in American English, it contributes to your non-native accent. If there's too much tension, the result will be choppy sounding speech with unnecessary pauses. Remember when we talked about how the rhythm and intonation of your first language results in accented English speech? The same thing goes for your voice. Unless you are able to relax and speak with the American voice quality, your speech will continue to be perceived as accented.

As you practice your sounds and intonation, keep reminding yourself to relax, and remember to reduce the tension in your throat, lips, and tongue. Think of keeping your speech forward in your mouth to avoid creating tension in your mouth cavity. When rehearsing your words and sentences, it is a good idea to record yourself so you can listen to the sound quality of your spoken American English. If your speech appears choppy, you're probably speaking with too much facial tension.

Reducing Facial Tension

Now that you know that Americans use very little tension when they speak, it will be to your advantage to take a look at the following exercises to relax or minimize any tension that may exist.

1. While you are in front of a mirror, relax and let your tongue stick out. With your mouth open, extend your tongue as far as possible, then relax. Push your tongue as hard as you can against the roof of your mouth, then relax. Then push your tongue to the floor of your mouth as hard as possible, and relax.

2. Slowly roll your head three or four times in one direction. Then do it again, the same number of times, in the opposite direction.

3. Open your mouth as wide as possible and relax. Purse your lips in an exaggerated pout, and then relax.

Oral Motor Exercises

The following exercises will benefit you regardless of your accent. The more flexible your tongue becomes, the easier it will be for you to maneuver from one sound to the next. In addition, some exercises focus on other parts of your speech mechanism. A combination of all these exercises will result in more articulate speech.

1. Tap your tongue five times on the roof of your mouth.

2. Stick your tongue out, and then pull it back in again five times.

3. Stick your tongue out as far as it will go, then draw it back into your mouth and touch the fleshy part toward the back of your throat, the soft palate.

4. Looking in a mirror, open your mouth and say "ah." Make sure your tongue is flat and you can see as far to the back of your throat as possible. Repeat several times.

5. With your mouth wide open, say the syllable "ka." Then say "ga." Watch the action in the back of your throat as your tongue touches your soft palate.

6. Open and close your mouth.

7. Pucker your lips as if you're whistling, then relax. Repeat.

8. Stretch your lips in an exaggerated smile and say "EEE." Then relax. Do that five times.

9. Pucker your lips and swing left, then swing right. Repeat.

10. Puff out your cheeks and hold the air, then slowly let the air out.

11. Push the inside of your cheek out with your tongue—first on the right side, then on the left side.

12. With your mouth slightly open, move your tongue from the right corner of your mouth to the left corner. Repeat three times.

The Least You Need to Know

◆ Grouping words into thought groups makes it easier for the speaker to compose a message and for the listener to understand it.

◆ Word groups are separated by pauses, which calls attention to the thought group and gives the speaker a moment to breathe.

◆ A controlled rate of speech is important and affects how you are perceived and understood.

◆ Americans use very little tension in their speech musculature when speaking.

◆ Oral motor exercises can help reduce facial tension and improve the flexibility of the speech articulators.

Part 3

Pronunciation: Consonant Troublemakers

Now that you are more comfortable with American English intonation, it's time to deal with the individual components that make up the melody. Think of consonants as the building blocks of American English words. But being familiar with them and being able to use them comfortably in your conversational speech are two different things. You certainly speak some of these consonants as if they were old friends. But there are other consonants that may be completely new to you, or maybe you are used to pronouncing them just differently enough that they alert people to your accented speech or get in the way of your being understood.

As you look through this part, don't be intimidated. You need to remember that Part 3 addresses all the consonants that cause difficulty for everyone who has grown up speaking a language other than English, with a special emphasis on the consonants that cause the most trouble. Your consonant nightmare is included. Ready to go in and do battle? Finally, those consonants have met their match.

Chapter 6

Speech Production 101

In This Chapter

◆ The intricate nature of speaking

◆ How we make speech sounds

◆ The nature of voiced and voiceless sounds

If you're anything like me, you get in the car, turn on the ignition, and drive to the supermarket without giving much thought to how you got there and back home again. Many of us take things for granted, I guess. It's not important how things work, just that they do.

But there are times when we need to take a more scientific approach and become more curious. When learning to modify an accent, it's essential to discover how you speak in the first place. Verbal communication seems simple enough. We open our mouths, words come out, and people respond to what we say. But when you look closely, you begin to see how truly extraordinary the art of speaking is. It is, in fact, among the subtlest and most distinctive actions performed by human beings.

How We Talk the Talk

It all begins when air is exhaled from the lungs. It's this air that gives you the energy to create the sounds of speech. The air passes from the lungs to the larynx, which contains the vocal cords. The vocal cords vibrate to produce a specific quality of sound. They can also tense or relax, and your voice will respond in a higher or lower pitch. After the air passes through the vocal cords, it is shaped into specific sounds and tones by the articulators—your tongue, teeth, jaw, lips, soft and hard palates, and the roof of your mouth. Adding to your own distinct vocal quality are your nose, mouth, and throat, acting as resonating chambers. If you want to speak louder or softer, your brain directs your lungs to increase or decrease the amount of air that passes through the entire vocal system.

Correct speech involves precise movements of the articulators that are shown here.

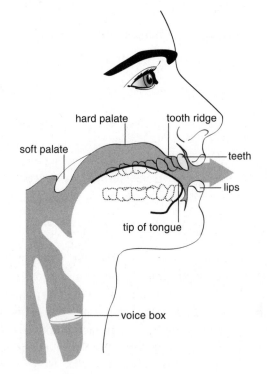

The Main Players

Think of the speech articulators as actors in a Broadway production. Although there are major and minor players, each character must be ready when the director (the brain) calls "Action!" These players also play a critical role in your own speech performance.

The tongue is the most visible and active performer due to its mobility and flexibility. Without it, you would have to shut down the entire show. Your speech would be unintelligible. But even though the tongue may be the most important member of the cast, it never makes an appearance without a supporting player. It continually taps and touches other articulators to create certain distinct sounds and to direct the flow of air to specific locations.

The teeth work with the lips and with the tongue to form sounds. Make the sound that the letter *f* stands for—fff. As you do, you feel your upper teeth connect with your lower lip. In some instances, the teeth form a wall to mark out the inner boundary of the mouth and to control airflow. And you thought all they could do was chew.

The tooth ridge, officially known as the alveolar ridge, contains the sockets of your teeth. You can feel this ridge with your tongue in the area right behind the top teeth. Make the sound that the letter *t* stands for and you'll be touching this ridge with your tongue.

The lips play a versatile role in the production. Though your upper and lower lip often work as a team, as when producing the sounds represented by *p* and *b*, the lips sometimes partner with other articulators such as the teeth. Remember the lower lip's memorable performance in fff? The lips also act as doorkeepers; they control the amount of air expelled from the mouth and they work to maneuver that air into distinctive sound patterns.

The hard palate is considered a supporting player because it can't do much on its own and has to wait for a cue from the tongue. You can feel the bones of your hard palate on the roof of your mouth. In addition to being a sounding board, it forms a partition between your mouth and nasal passages.

The soft palate is the continuation of the hard palate as it extends deeper into your mouth. You can feel this fleshy extension where the hard palate blends into the soft palate by stretching your tongue toward the back of your mouth. The interaction between the tongue and the soft palate is essential for the formation of certain sounds. Unlike the hard palate, the soft palate is moveable and is responsible for closing off the nasal passages when swallowing or shutting off air to the nose.

> **Info-Nugget**
>
> Speech is more complicated than you think. To produce a spoken phrase, about 100 muscles of the chest, neck, jaw, tongue, and lips must collaborate.

Cue the Vocal Cords

Refer to the illustration of the speech mechanism earlier in this chapter and see where the vocal cords are. As you can see, the diagram shows the voice box, or larynx, at the top of the windpipe. Inside the voice box are the vocal cords, which are small muscular folds on each side of the larynx. When air passes between these folds, they vibrate—or not, depending on what the brain tells them to do. That's something that is critical for you to know as you try to change your accent. For some sounds, the vocal cords vibrate; for others, they don't.

As you probably already know, our speech sounds are divided into vowels and consonants. All vowels are voiced. So whenever you say a vowel, the vocal cords are vibrating. Consonants, however, are either voiced or voiceless. We produce voiced consonant sounds with vibration of the vocal cords, and we produce voiceless, or unvoiced, consonant sounds by simply passing air through the vocal cords.

Let's take the sound fff, for example—the sound that the letter *f* stands for. It's the first sound in the word *fun*. Your upper teeth are placed on your lower lip, and air travels up from your lungs through your vocal cords. However, the vocal cords do not vibrate. The air that exits your mouth when you say fff is simply that—air.

Try it yourself. Make one long fff sound and at the same time put your hand on your throat over your larynx. You shouldn't feel any vibration because *f* is a voiceless, or unvoiced, consonant.

Now *f* has a partner, so to speak. It's the sound that the letter *v* represents. It's the first sound in *vanilla*. Say the word and stretch out the first sound—vvv. Put your hand over your larynx and make the sound again. This time you will feel vibration because *v* is a voiced consonant.

Stumbling Block

The fleshy appendage that dangles from the back of your throat is called the uvula, and it's an extension of the soft palate. Touching it evokes a strong gag reflex in most people. Don't do it.

Did you notice any parallel between the two sounds? The sounds for *f* and *v* are produced the same way. The teeth and lips were in the same position for both sounds. The only difference was that for the *v*'s sound the vocal cords vibrated, and for the *f*'s sound they didn't.

Why is this so important? Because this is a common error that non-native English speakers make. They find themselves voicing a sound that shouldn't be voiced, or vice versa. This pattern of voiced and voiceless consonants occurs consistently throughout the English language, and you need to have a firm handle on which is which. Because this is such a widespread problem, we'll go over it in greater detail in the next chapter.

The Least You Need to Know

◆ Speech is the result of a series of precisely coordinated muscle movements.

◆ The speech mechanism includes primarily the tongue, teeth, lips, jaw, hard and soft palates, and the vocal cords.

◆ The tongue is the most important of the articulators due to its mobility and flexibility.

◆ Voiced sounds are produced when the vocal cords vibrate inside the voice box, or larynx.

◆ Unvoiced sounds are produced when air passes through the vocal cords, but the cords do not vibrate.

Most Common Consonant Problems

In This Chapter

- ◆ Focusing on common yet troublesome problems
- ◆ Discovering ways to overcome some consonant errors
- ◆ Learning why omitting sounds is a common habit
- ◆ Crunching two sounds into one

There is a wide variety of consonant sounds in American English. Many of them exist in your native language but may be produced in a slightly different way. There are others that you may never have heard before you began to learn English. But even if you are familiar with all the consonants, you may still find that you are having problems incorporating a few of them into your everyday speech. For some reason, they just don't sound right to you.

There's a good chance that the problem you are having is addressed in this chapter. Of all the problems that non-native speakers have with American English, the issues covered in this chapter cause the greatest difficulty. Rather than deal with specific sound problems, this chapter deals with general speech behaviors. It's important information that could lead to a major breakthrough. There's a good chance that your speech is much better than you think it is. After you discover your problem area, you may find that all you need to sound more American is to make a few minor adjustments.

Voiced and Voiceless Mix-Ups

In some languages, the difference between voiced and unvoiced sounds is not important—but it is important in American English. A common error that many non-native English speakers make is that they turn off their vocal cords when they should be using them—and vice versa. The problem occurs most frequently at the ends of words. When someone produces a voiceless sound when it should be voiced, it's like missing a beat in a sentence. It may, in fact, result in creating an entirely different word.

If voicing certain consonants is a new skill for you, it may feel awkward at first, but with practice and determination, you should be able to acquire the voiced-voiceless switch without too much difficulty.

Track 11: Let's see if I can make this clearer. On the top row of the table that follows are letters and letter combinations that represent voiceless sounds. Underneath each voiceless sound are letters that represent its voiced counterpart. I've demonstrated these differences for you on the CD. To make it easier for you, I suggest you follow along.

Voiceless:	p	t	f	k	s	sh	ch	th
Voiced:	b	d	v	g	z	zh	dj	TH

Now listen to the sounds in word pairs. Each word in the first column ends in a voiceless sound. Each word in the second column ends in the voiced counterpart of the first word's final sound.

cup	cub
seat	seed
half	have
flack	flag
cease	seize
bath	bathe
bus	buzz

To compare voiceless SH and CH sounds and voiced ZH and DJ sounds, you must listen carefully. As with other voiceless and voiced sounds, both sounds are produced the same way, but the vocal cords vibrate only for the voiced sound.

Voiceless SH:	She shot the sheriff with a shotgun.
	Marsha put on lotion and went to the ocean.
Voiced ZH:	The Asian and Caucasian sat on a Persian rug.
	Take pleasure in the vision of your treasure.
	Jacques made a decision to give up long division.
Voiceless CH:	Blanche chewed chunky chicken for lunch.
	Charlie the butcher was on crutches in church.
Voiced DJ:	The Judge gave the jury many pages to digest.
	January, June, and July are my favorite months.

 Stumbling Block

Vibrating your vocal cords at the wrong time can result in a different word than you had intended. You need to know which sounds are voiceless and which are voiced not only for proper pronunciation but to convey your meaning.

Omitting Final Sounds

Just as non-native American English speakers have a tendency not to voice sounds at the ends of words, many have a habit of omitting final sounds entirely. The reason is that many words in many languages do not end with consonant sounds.

It's easy to understand why this can cause so much difficulty. Some languages end in open-mouth vowel sounds. French speakers are used to silent consonants at the ends of words. Russians use smooth yet slurring connections between words, and Asian speakers are used to sound stability and are *not* used to changeable word endings. All these result in major habits to overcome.

The first step in correcting sound omissions is to make an effort to hear the sounds that are being omitted. In other words, you need to find out what sounds you are leaving out of your speech.

If you haven't identified the missing sound or sounds when you recorded your speech sample, ask a native-born American speaker to help you to analyze your speech and let you know if and when you are omitting sounds. Read the speech sample with your mentor listening. If your mentor indicates that you are missing a sound, underline all the words that include that particular sound. Of course, you aren't limited to the speech sample. Any short passage will do. Then head for Carnegie Hall—and practice, practice, practice.

Sound Advice

If you find that you are omitting sounds, practice and exercise are essential. Physical exercises will help, too. Chapter 5 offers many exercises to choose from.

Substituting Sounds

As you are aware, the reason you have an accent is that you are accustomed to the rhythm, stresses, and sounds of your native language. And although some sounds in American English are the same as those in your first language, your natural tendency when you come to an English sound with which you are unfamiliar is to default to a sound that you are used to pronouncing. The problem is that the sound you're using as a substitute might not be close enough to American English and may sound like accented speech to an American.

Here's an example: English uses the TH sound frequently. It's a sound that's not present in every language. To a German-born native speaker, the closest familiar sound is T.

That's his default sound. So he might pronounce *threw* as *true* and *three* as *tree*. You can see how this could get confusing. Of course, the context of what you are saying will help the listener understand, but there is the possibility that some listeners may not decipher your message correctly.

> **Info-Nugget**
>
> Your English pronunciation is probably better than you think. On average, there are only five or six sounds that are not common between English and other languages.

Rather than give you a list of which sounds are most commonly substituted for other sounds, it will be more meaningful for you to deal with your own individual sound errors. Find the sounds that are causing you trouble in the upcoming sections. Included with each sound are instructions on how to produce the sound correctly, along with the common sound substitutions.

Consonant Blends or Clusters

Regardless of what you want to call them, blends or clusters, they are the same thing. A consonant blend or cluster is a group of consonants without any vowels between them. Consonant clusters occur in all positions in words: beginning (*clam*, *stop*), middle (*proclaim*, *piston*), and end (*consist*, *cold*). Many different consonants appear in clusters.

When reading clusters, the letter sounds within the cluster combine to form one sound. Even though you can hear each sound, they are so tightly crunched as to sound like one. Take the word *band*, for example. How many distinct sounds do you hear? Actually, the answer is three because *n* and *d* combine to form one sound.

Pronouncing these consonant clusters or blends may feel awkward at first, but with active listening and practice you will catch on quickly.

It's important for you to be aware of the common errors that some non-native English speakers make when it comes to consonant blends. After you know about them, you can avoid them yourself.

1. There is a tendency to de-voice the last sound in the blend. Instead of vibrating the vocal cords for the last sound, it becomes a voiceless sound. For example, instead of *band*, it comes out *bant*. Or instead of *told*, it comes out *tolt*.

2. Sometimes people treat a consonant blend as two separate sounds. For example, instead of saying *blue*, it comes out as "buh-lue." And *clown* would incorrectly be "cuh-lown."

3. It's common for people to mispronounce SK as KS, especially in the word *ask*, which is mispronounced as "aks."

The Least You Need to Know

◆ A common speech error is using a voiceless sound instead of a voiced sound at the ends of words.

◆ Substituting one sound for another is a common habit, especially if the new sound does not occur in your native language.

◆ Omitting sounds from words not only makes your speech sound more accented, but also interferes with conveying your meaning.

◆ Consonant blends or clusters occur at the beginnings, middles, and ends of words. The two consonant sounds blend into one sound.

Chapter 8

Two Big Consonant Troublemakers

In This Chapter

- ◆ Meeting two consonant archenemies
- ◆ Learning how to produce these consonant sounds correctly
- ◆ Practicing the correct sounds in words and sentences

If it's any consolation, you're not alone in struggling with the "bad boys" in this chapter. Talk to a speech pathologist in any school in America, and you will find that a good part of his or her caseload is made up of students who have difficulty with these sounds. Even some adults who have been speaking English since childhood don't make all these sounds correctly.

You may not be having trouble with all these troublemakers, but mispronouncing just one can make your speech sound more accented. The key is to select your target sound, listen for the way it is correctly produced, and practice the corrected sound in words and sentences until you can proudly show it off in your conversational speech.

The Thorny TH

Phonetic Symbol: th voiceless /θ/
                         TH voiced /ð/

Without a doubt, the TH sound is one of the most challenging for non-native English speakers. Chances are good that it wasn't a part of your native language and your brain has tuned it out. Now you need to work harder to hear it, distinguish it from all the other sounds of American English, and determine its unique characteristics.

But there's more to consider. Not only is the TH sound different, it is produced differently from how other sounds are produced. It is the only sound for which your tongue actually goes beyond your teeth. When you attempt it, it will probably feel awkward. But all new habits feel strange at first.

Voiceless and Voiced Versions of TH

There are two versions of the TH sound, voiceless and voiced. To recap: A voiceless sound is made without the vocal cords vibrating; a voiced sound requires vocal cords to vibrate. To complicate matters, both versions of TH are spelled the same way. To make this simpler for teaching purposes, I'll refer to voiceless th in lowercase letters and the voiced version as TH.

Notice how the tongue extends beyond the teeth.

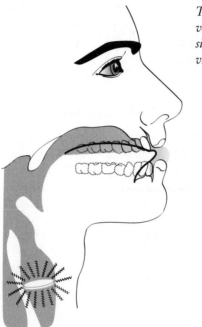

The difference between the voiceless and voiced versions is that your vocal cords vibrate with voiced TH.

Take a look at the th and TH illustrations. Notice that the only difference is the vocal cords vibrate for TH.

How You Do It: Voiceless th

To produce a proper voiceless th sound, it may help you to envision a snake's tongue. The tip of your tongue is tense and darts out between your teeth very quickly and then snaps back in again. You need to keep your mouth slightly open so there's just enough space to place the tip of your tongue between your upper and lower teeth. Flatten the tip of your tongue and let it touch the upper teeth. Then push a voiceless stream of air over the tongue. Remember this is just a stream of air. If you place your hand over your throat you should not feel a vibration from the vocal cords.

How You Do It: Voiced TH

The voiced version of TH is produced the same way. Your teeth, lips, and tongue do the same thing. This time, though, when you push air, you cause the vocal cords to vibrate. If you find that the sound isn't loud enough, you might find it helpful to have a bit more tongue tension with light contact between your tongue and your upper teeth. Remember that this sound has some duration to it, so don't cut it short.

Listening Practice: Voiceless th and Voiced TH

Track 12: Here are some examples that will help you hear the voiceless th at the beginning, middle, and ends of words. I will pronounce each one on the CD. For now, just listen.

Voiceless th

Beginning:	thunder	thought	thrilling	think
Middle:	bathtub	Catholic	faithful	birthday
End:	bath	worth	mirth	moth

Voiced TH

Beginning:	them	that	then	there
Middle:	mother	feather	weather	teething
End:	bathe	soothe	breathe	teethe

Common Mistakes

Because both the voiceless th and voiced TH sounds are used frequently in American English, producing the sound incorrectly will be noticeable and will be perceived as part of a non-native accent. If you are having difficulty with either sound, it could be that you are substituting another sound in its place. A common error is to use T instead of voiceless th. Others say D instead of the voiced TH. Another error is that the tongue may not be placed far enough beyond the teeth and it sounds more like a whistling or S or Z sound.

Here's the Drill: Voiceless th

Now it's your turn. Practice these words carefully and be sure to position your tongue between your teeth as you begin each word.

through	thermometer
three	thrilling
thimble	theater
thigh	thesaurus

Pronouncing the voiceless th sound at the end of a word is your next step. Be sure that your tongue is extended beyond your teeth and that you're not making the T sound by mistake.

broth	mirth
bath	death
mouth	with
oath	breath

When you feel you are ready to tackle the voiceless th sound in the middle of a word, it will feel the most awkward. Your tongue pops out after one sound and then pops back in so you can make another sound. Just remember—all of America is doing it!

bathroom	method
Catholic	Lutheran
earthquake	gothic
birthday	faithful

The following sentences all contain words with the voiceless th sound. Read each sentence slowly and carefully at first. When you feel more comfortable, deliver the sentence without looking at it using the rules of good American intonation.

1. Anthony was thrilled when he saw the panther.

2. Timothy was thirsty on Thursday because he lost his thermos.

3. Thelma thought you had to be wealthy to go to the theater.

4. I'll be with you through thick and thin.

5. After her bath, Beth asked for a toothbrush and toothpaste.

Here's the Drill—Voiced TH

Get ready to practice the voiced TH. Make sure your vocal cords are vibrating and your tongue is outside your mouth at the *beginning* of each word.

that	they
there	therefore
them	the
this	then

Voiced TH is at the ends of the following words. When practicing, give it a little extra energy. You can always tone it down in natural conversation.

soothe	bathe
breathe	smooth
seethe	lathe
teethe	soothe

Producing the voiced TH sound in the middle of a word is probably the most difficult. Make sure you feel confident in the previous word positions before tackling this one.

rather	heathen
weather	leather
bathing	soothing
mother	wither

The following sentences will help you practice using the voiced TH with more of a conversational tone.

1. The baby was teething though father was soothing.
2. Don't bother Mother when she's bathing.
3. The flowers withered because they weren't watered.
4. They told us that the feathers were theirs.
5. I'd rather have this one than that one.

Advanced Practice

All sentences here contain both voiceless th and voiced TH. I didn't underline the letters for you this time. If it helps you, go ahead and underline or circle each occurrence of *th* yourself. There is no general rule to help you determine which *th* is voiced and which is voiceless. That's why you need a good dictionary!

1. I thought that Mother wanted a leather throne.
2. Father said we need to bathe whether we like it or not.
3. I think that I would rather live in the south than the north.
4. Catherine loathes this kind of weather.
5. It was thoughtful of you to stay during the thunderstorm.
6. Theo studied theology for three years at Catholic University.
7. The thief stole thousands of worthless feathers.
8. Give it to them before they alert the authorities.
9. They bathed again even though they had washed on Thursday.
10. Heather and Father are sympathetic with the author's view.

The Elusive L

Phonetic Symbol: /l/

Though some non-native English speakers may be able to produce a correct L sound in some words, they may not be as successful when the

L is in certain word positions. You should note that although there is a slight difference in the position of the tongue for the various word positions of L, the differences are so subtle that to concentrate on them here would not result in any major breakthrough. Instead, we will focus on a standard L sound and use it in all word positions. When you become more comfortable with the sound and its usage, you will adjust to the more subtle adjustments automatically.

The L sound requires a precise placement of the tongue tip behind the upper teeth.

How You Do It

To make the L sound, pretend as if you are making a T sound. Do you feel where your tongue is placed? That's the exact spot from which you will "launch" the L. Keep the contact between your tongue and your gum ridge light because you will be making a flicking tongue motion, not lengthy contact. But remember, the L sound is a voiced consonant.

Common Mistakes

There are varieties of errors that people make when producing the L sound. Some substitute other sounds, such as W and R, or use too much force or tongue pressure. The L sound can be distorted if the back of the tongue touches the soft palate. Another common error is omitting the sound altogether.

To help improve tongue flexibility, see Chapter 5 and the section on oral motor exercises. This will help improve the mobility of your tongue for this and other sounds. Another good tool to use is a mirror so you can observe your tongue in the correct L position on the gum ridge behind your upper teeth.

Listening Practice

Track 13: To modify a speech pattern, you first need to hear it and identify it in your everyday speech. With that in mind, listen to this section on the CD. Hear the correct pronunciation of the L sound in all positions in words. Then repeat them after me.

Beginning:	lace	Latin	leaf	letter
Middle:	elephant	sailor	relent	color
End:	battle	cool	seagull	popsicle

Here's the Drill: L

Now put what you've heard into practice. Remember to start with your tongue behind your gum ridge and lightly make the L sound while moving your tongue tip down into the sound that follows. Be sure to relax your tongue. Let's start with the L sound in the beginning position.

list	lotion
locomotive	laminate
lovely	legislate
lap	lemon

1. The lovely lady led me here.

2. Lucy was lucky that Larry was late.

3. Luke was a lawyer before he was a legislator.

4. Lazy Lester was lounging.

5. I lost your lovely lace scarf.

When the L sound is the last sound that you hear in a word, your tongue remains in the L position with no other sound following it.

mule	puddle
fool	model
school	rail
all	small

1. Bill paid the bail and got out of jail.

2. I had some ale with my awful meal.

3. Gail will fail in school.

4. My goal is to scale a mountain this April.

5. I feel full after eating all the veal.

When the L sound is in a middle position, keep your tongue flexible and maintain a light touch to accommodate sounds that occur before and after the L sound.

follow	lollipop
mellow	pillow
million	railroad
gallows	rally

1. We saw a million alligators in Florida.

2. Sally followed her fellow to Kalamazoo.

3. Jolly Molly gave all the kids lollipops.

4. Carla put her silver bracelet with her other jewelry.

5. The sailor gave Dolly a yellow blouse.

Advanced Practice

The L sound is in a variety of word positions in these practice sentences. Underlining the letter *l* where it occurs in these words may help you pronounce the words correctly.

1. The lawyer led the evil lady to the gallows last April.

2. It is illegal to peel lemons in the library in July.

3. Larry blamed Lucy for losing his golf game in Florida.

4. We went to the mall after school to buy a plaid umbrella.

5. Lucinda took the blame for causing all the trouble.

6. Clarence took his model locomotive to school.

7. Linda found her lace camisole before the holidays.

8. The crystal glasses on the table looked clean.

9. It is lunacy to ride a mule a mile to school.

10. The lanky linesman played football in college.

The Least You Need to Know

◆ TH is the only sound in English whose production involves extending your tongue beyond your teeth.

◆ The TH sound is always spelled with the letters *th*, whether the sound is voiced or voiceless.

◆ To find the exact place to make the L sound, start to make a T and then keep your tongue on that place on the roof of your mouth.

Chapter 9

Two More Big Consonant Troublemakers

In This Chapter

- ◆ Meeting S and Z up close and personal
- ◆ Standing up to the R sound!
- ◆ Learning techniques to conquer them all

Just when you thought you had wrestled the biggest trouble-makers into submission, along comes another chapter that introduces you to a few more. But don't get discouraged! You already have the formula for better pronunciation. First, study how the sound is made, then listen carefully as I demonstrate the sounds in words. Then practice, practice, practice! Before you know it, you'll wonder why you ever called these sounds troublesome.

The Prickly Pair: S and Z

Phonetic Symbols: /s/ and /z/

It's time to meet another pair of sounds—S and Z. They're a couple with a difference. S is unvoiced; Z is voiced. Many American children have trouble pronouncing these sounds and sometimes need speech therapy to overcome the difficulty. By the time they reach adulthood, however, most Americans produce the sounds correctly.

Tongue placement is critical for the correct production of the S and Z sounds.

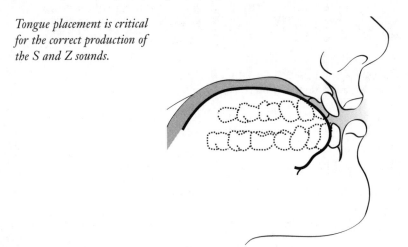

How You Do It

Sometimes, explaining how to produce a sound is more difficult than actually producing it. That's why I encourage you to pay close attention when I demonstrate the examples for both the S and Z sounds. Some people catch on just by hearing the two sounds and imitating what they hear.

For those who learn better with written instructions, however, here they are: the S sound is produced with minimal space between the top and bottom front teeth; the sides of the tongue are high against the upper back teeth. The air moves down the groove in your tongue and goes through the narrow space between the teeth and the tongue. The S sound is a long sound, not a quick one. Z, as the voiced counterpart of S, is also a long sound. Tongue and teeth placement should be identical for the two sounds, except that the vocal cords vibrate for Z and they do not vibrate for S.

Common Mistakes

Many non-native English speakers have difficulty with the S and Z sounds. There are several reasons why:

1. Many people can produce a moderate approximation but never hit it right on the mark. In other words, they come close but do not make the clean, crisp sounds that are necessary to be perceived as being non-accented.

2. Some accented speakers place their tongue in the wrong position and the S or Z is perceived as being thick or sloppy.

3. The biggest problem arises in distinguishing between the S and Z sounds and learning when to use one instead of the other. Many non-native speakers substitute the S sound for the voiced Z sound.

4. Some speakers completely eliminate the sound, hoping that no one will notice. Trust me, people will. We will address all these problems in this chapter.

Listening Practice

Track 14: To conquer this sound, first listen to it carefully in all the word examples on the CD. After you listen, I will leave time for you to repeat the word. Try to come as close as you can to produce a correct sound.

Beginning:	soap	silly	spot	sack
Middle:	castle	rascal	missile	impossible
End:	miss	face	Dallas	glass

Beginning:	zoo	zephyr	Zachary	zither
Middle:	misery	easy	lazy	pleasant
End:	lose	eyes	please	noise

Here's the Drill: S

First you will practice the S sound when it is the first sound in a word. Remember, the vocal cords are not vibrating and we should not see your tongue. As you will notice, *c* can also represent the S sound in words.

soap	center
salty	civil
school	several
special	speech

In the following words, S is the very last sound. Both *s* and *c* represent the S sound in these words.

Dallas	thanks
Venice	goose
chalice	juice
lass	cats

Now the S sound is in the middle, between other sounds. This is the most difficult position. Again, notice that both *s* and *c* represent the S sound.

massive	register
mustard	postal
master	icy
dusty	roasted

The following sentences include words that contain the S sound in all positions. Use what you have been learning to create the correct intonational rhythm along with the correct articulation of S.

1. The science seminar lasted all day.

2. The forecast is for snow and ice on Saturday.

3. Sally spent sixty-six dollars for her spelling books.

4. It's nice when you get first-class service.

5. Practicing speech on a regular basis gets best results.

6. Thanks so much for the silver bracelet and necklace.

7. The waitress provided exceptional service at the restaurant.

8. Students say that the best time of day is recess.

9. My daughter Kristin studied many subjects at the university.

10. The crossing guard helped Missy get across the street.

Here's the Drill: Z

There are very few words in English that begin with the Z sound. The few that do almost all begin with the letter *z*. Watch out, though, for the occasional initial *x*; it has the Z sound, too.

zoo	zenith
zeal	zebra
xylophone	zephyr

Next, practice some words that end in the Z sound. In these words, the ending may be spelled with an *s* or *z*, but it is pronounced with the Z sound. Remember, the Z sound is always voiced.

is	eyes
melons	prize
knows	analyze
clothes	fries

The hardest place to pronounce the Z sound is in the middle of a word. Again, either *s* or *z* may represent the Z sound.

music	hazy
buzzing	buzzard
crazy	daisy
frazzled	easy

Using the Z sound correctly in spontaneous speech begins with using the correct sound in sentence practice.

1. The lazy lizard disguised himself as a buzzard.

2. Daisy said the music was driving her crazy.

3. Maisie visited Zurich on Wednesday.

4. Zach says that razor is rusty.

5. Sam and Zachary sold melons to the ladies in the street.

6. Smoking is a hazard to healthy lungs.

7. First Sam was analyzed and then he was hypnotized.

8. They were dazzled when they saw the grizzly at the zoo.

9. Classical music always makes me dizzy.

10. Zoe closed her eyes and thought about the prize.

Advanced Practice

Ready for a bigger challenge? The following sentences contain both the S and Z sounds in all word positions. There are no hints, so you need to figure it out for yourself. But here's a reminder: The letter *s* is not the only letter that represents the S sound.

1. The boys went to baseball practice for the big game on Sunday.

2. The circus ringmaster announced that we would see the Greatest Show on Earth!

3. This silk blouse feels very soft against my skin.

4. Sally's sister took us to the zoo on Tuesday.

5. The boys got blisters from the strong rays of the sun.

6. Frozen waffles with syrup are my favorite breakfast.

7. Zoey told Sally that she was crazy for taking such a risk.

8. Melissa bought raisins, pineapples, apples, and grapes for her salad.

9. I want a 16-ounce sirloin steak, extra juicy and sizzling!

10. My sister Suzy spends lots of time sewing socks for soldiers.

The Dreaded R

Phonetic Symbol: /ɪ/

I have no doubt that some people would like to nominate the R sound as a contender for America's most troublesome sound. This is a sound like no other. Though other versions of the sound exist in other languages, no version is quite like ours. It's an identity problem, really. It's classified as a consonant, but when connected to certain vowels, the sound changes just enough to be thought of as a semi-vowel. How strong and obvious the R sound is has to do with how close it is to a vowel. To be perfectly honest, the differences between all the R sounds is minimal and is difficult to hear. My advice is to learn how to produce the R sound as a consonant. When you can do that easily, you can practice it in different words and discover the subtle changes.

How You Do It

Pronouncing the R sound requires a precise oral motor movement, but there is no tactile feedback. In other words, I can tell you how to produce the sound, but giving you exact directions is difficult because I'll be describing a movement rather than a specific position of the tongue. Pronouncing the R sound involves taking your tongue back toward your throat and arching it at the same time. Look at the illustration. It may help to think tip up, tongue back, voice box on. Your lips pucker slightly.

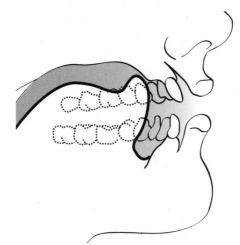

It takes lots of practice to perfect the R sound.

Common Mistakes

In many other languages, the R sound is produced by keeping the lips flat and placing the tip of the tongue just behind the upper front teeth, so that it sounds like a very quick D or several quick D sounds together. This is often called "trilling." Because other R sounds differ from the American English R, listeners often need time to process the difference. Some non-native English speakers—especially those of Asian-Pacific origin—have the tendency to drop the R sound in their speech. When a sound substitution occurs, speakers are likely to use the W sound in place of R.

Listening Practice

Track 15: The R sound is a difficult sound for many to hear. Pay close attention as I pronounce the R sound on the CD in different word positions.

Beginning:	robot	raisin	roof	radio
Middle:	carry	Earth	word	learn
End:	over	wonder	mister	feather

Here's the Drill: R

Try to make the sound on its own. If it's not coming easily, try saying eeee and then moving to rrrr. After you successfully make the sound, incorporate it into the words in these practice lists. First, say these words that begin with the R sound.

radish	regal
rodeo	royal
remain	Rhode Island
Rome	raisin

As you pronounce the R sound at the ends of words, make sure the tip of your tongue is not in contact with the roof of your mouth.

father	dinner
mother	plumber
daughter	teacher
fighter	inquire

Try the R sound in the middle of words. Because this is the most difficult position in which to pronounce the R sound correctly, practice this list several times.

carriage	blueberry
profit	verbal
tolerate	charming
wonderful	thrilling

Advanced Practice

The R sound is in a variety of word positions in these practice sentences. Underlining the letter wherever it occurs may help you pronounce it correctly in each word.

1. Rainbows regularly appear in Richmond.

2. The roosters were roaming around the ranch yesterday.

3. Read the story about Red Ranger.

4. Little Red Riding Hood visited Grandma's house.

5. Randy ordered broiled lobster at the restaurant.

6. Write a letter to your mother for her birthday.

7. Did you remember to wrap the present for your sister?

8. President Obama was inaugurated in January.

9. The ruby ring cost forty-four dollars and thirty-three cents.

10. Father told Mother about the surprise cruise to Aruba.

The Least You Need to Know

◆ Be careful when you see an *s* at the end of a word. Sometimes it makes the S sound and sometimes it makes the Z sound.

◆ Remember not to confuse the S sound with TH. If you stick your tongue out when making the S sound, it will quickly revert to the TH sound.

◆ To produce the R sound, make sure that the tip of your tongue is not touching any part of your mouth.

◆ Because R is a difficult sound, you may experience faster progress by first listening for the sound before actually trying to pronounce it.

Chapter 10

Ready for Some Explosive Sounds?

In This Chapter

- ◆ Understanding the explosive nature of the P and B sounds
- ◆ Getting two-for-one with the T and D sounds
- ◆ Using the back of the tongue for the K and G sounds

This chapter is all about power. Power that you probably didn't even realize you had. It's the power to create mini-sound explosions in your mouth and fire them at will. How? By adding them to whatever word you choose. Linguists call them "plosives." Making these sounds involves building up air pressure and then setting it free!

If you're having difficulty with any of the plosive sounds, this chapter will fix all that. The first step is to make sure you're hearing the sound correctly. Then we learn the way it should be produced and practice the correct sound until it becomes a habit.

A Little Lip Action: P and B

Phonetic Symbols: /p/ and /b/

You probably don't have much trouble making these sounds. In fact, they're among the first ones babies make when they're in the babbling stage. But although I'm sure you won't have any difficulty producing the sounds, it's possible that you may use them at the wrong time, or you may apply more pressure than you need to. As you know, Americans don't use a lot of tension when we speak. So these mini-explosions should be given the same power or emphasis as the other sounds in your sentences. They're not intended to knock someone's sunglasses off!

How You Do It

To produce a proper P sound, put your lips together while tension builds up behind them. When you're ready to make the sound, you simply push that burst of air through your mouth. If you hold your hand in front of your mouth, you should feel a puff of air. The B sound is produced the same way, except the vocal cords vibrate.

It takes a light buildup of pressure to make both the P and B sounds.

Common Mistakes

There are a few areas that you should think about when creating these two sounds. One, as I just mentioned, is to be careful not to over-punch or over-deliver the sounds. You don't want these two plosives to be any more obvious than the other sounds you're speaking. The other thing to think about is to make sure that your P sound is heard, even though it is a voiceless sound.

Listening Practice

Track 16: Most English learners don't have too much trouble producing these sounds, or telling P apart from B. Listen to the CD to make sure you're on the right track.

Beginning:	pill	pea	poor	pay
Middle:	apple	report	carpet	upper
End:	keep	sharp	help	tape

Beginning:	book	better	before	buy
Middle:	rubber	number	rabbit	baby
End:	grab	tube	scrub	job

Here's the Drill: P

The best way to practice the P sound is to say words that begin with *p*. As you say each one, be sure that there's a buildup of pressure and that your vocal cords are not vibrating.

puzzle	pause
puddle	Poland
plastic	peaches
professor	Pakistan
pizza	palomino

When the P sound is at the end of a word, you may not need as much pressure as you did when P was in the initial position. Just make sure you don't drop this voiceless sound.

tulip	gallop
gallop	coop
develop	hope
sip	lump
shop	trump

Try the same sound in the middle of words. You will feel yourself building up the pressure and then just as quickly letting it go.

happy	apple
shopper	dripping
staple	napping
computer	whopper
pepper	campaign

Advanced Practice

Now it's time to put everything you have learned to good use in these sentences. First, read them aloud. Then memorize them and say them as if you are speaking, not reading. Remember to practice all the American intonation skills you have learned.

1. I ordered pepperoni pizza at the food plaza.

2. The reporter planned an update for the paper.

3. Pete bought flip-flops in the shop.

4. The complicated project involved paper and paste.

5. I hope the harpist performs at the party.

6. Peter Pan is my favorite play.

7. I plan to solve the puzzle and play the piano.

8. Please ask Papa if I can have a sip of cappuccino.

9. Pat was happy to get a new laptop computer.

10. Peter Piper picked a peck of pickled peppers.

Here's the Drill: B

Practice the B sound in the beginning position of words. Make sure you feel your vocal cords vibrating.

buckle	balloon
bingo	bongo
bistro	blister
browser	bandit
bell	broadcast

Now you need to practice the B sound at the end of the word. Note that when the sound is in this final position, it is not necessary to expel as much air as when the sound is in the initial position.

tub	scrub
cab	verb
knob	nightclub
stab	globe
job	crab

When *b* is in the middle of a word, get ready for the buildup of pressure and quick release of air before you move to the next sound.

laboratory	hobby
rabbit	cobble
trouble	label
remember	tubing
marble	liable

Advanced Practice

Read each sentence and underline where the B sound occurs. Then say each sentence. Finally, memorize a few of the sentences and say them as if they were part of a real conversation. Remember to stress key words for proper American style intonation.

1. I remember when Bob burned all the bacon.

2. Brenda and Billy took a bountiful basket to the beach.

3. I love lobster, melted butter, and baked potatoes the best.

4. The bathtub would benefit from a brisk scrubbing.

5. A big black bug bit a big black dog on his big black nose.

6. The bumblebees were busy buzzing.

7. After the bomb, there was nothing left but rubble.

8. Bradley finds the bookkeeping business quite boring.

9. Look in the basement for the baby's bunny rabbit.

10. Barack Obama is the first black president ever elected.

Learn Two at a Time: T and D

Phonetic Symbols: /t/ and /d/

There's nothing dramatically new to think about in making the T and D sounds. It's pretty much the same "buildup and release" process you used for the P and B sounds. Now, however, you must put the tongue in play. After you have learned the T sound, all you have to do is add a little voltage to your voice box and the D sound effortlessly occurs.

How You Do It

Form the T sound by placing the tip of the tongue on the gum ridge directly behind the upper teeth. When it touches, build up air pressure and then release both the tongue and the air pressure. Form the D sound the same way, except the vocal cords vibrate.

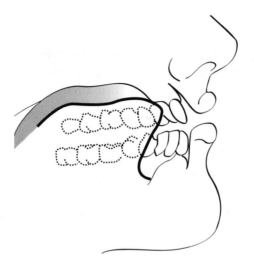

A light touch of the tongue is required for the T and D sounds.

Common Mistakes

As you know, you can't always rely on spelling to learn how to pronounce a word. Sometimes you just have to remember it.

♦ When the T sound occurs between two vowel sounds in an unstressed syllable, it is not pronounced as sharply as usual and sounds more like a D sound. This is called a "tapped T" and it doesn't require as much of a buildup of air. Examples: *metal, fatal.*

♦ In the past tense, when an "ed" ending is preceded by a voiceless sound, the "ed" is pronounced with a T sound. For example: *walked* and *jumped.* Because the *k* in *walked* and the *p* in *jumped* are voiceless sounds, the "ed" ending is pronounced with a voiceless T sound.

♦ When an "ed" ending is preceded by a voiced sound, the "ed" is pronounced with a D sound. For example: *paddled, hummed, shoved.* Because *l*, *m*, and *v* are voiced consonants, the "ed" ending is pronounced with a voiced D sound.

Listening Practice

Track 17: Listen to the CD as I demonstrate the two sounds for you in the context of words. Pay close attention to the differences between the T and D sounds. They can be very subtle.

Beginning:	time	train	two	town
Middle:	retail	after	rented	enter
End:	light	meet	chart	thought

Beginning:	dog	dollar	deal	dust
Middle:	address	poodle	meadow	louder
End:	read	food	pointed	covered

Here's the Drill: T

Practice the initial T sound in the following words. Feel your tongue touch the gum ridge before you let the air out.

toy	taffy
truck	technical
toad	tickle
telephone	tailor
terrible	tower

Practice the T sound at the end of a word. Note that when the sound is in this final position, it is not necessary to expel as much air. In fact, some Americans don't expel air when the tongue reaches the gum ridge.

president	gloat
draft	about
crust	habit
aircraft	basket
roost	seat

When *t* is in the middle of a word, you will feel your tongue move to the gum ridge before the sound is spoken.

Italy	butterfly
bitter	letter
butter	bottle
fatter	article
cheater	curtain

Advanced Practice

Here's an opportunity to test the T sound in all positions and to practice your intonation at the same time. Remember to stress key words as you first read, then say these sentences in a manner that sounds like natural conversation.

1. The Democrats in the Senate voted against the hotly contested bill.

2. Have you ever tasted chocolate gelato in Italy?

3. Be certain that you articulate every sound in the sentence.

4. The fat actor tore down the tapestry in the tower.

5. Terry ordered a triple latte and it gave him the jitters.

6. It was drafty in Vermont and I forgot my sweater.

7. Teresa said she would not tolerate Tony's cheating.

8. The actor who played Hamlet was tall and talented.

9. Robert has a habit of talking to strangers on the street.

10. Tom put the message in the bottle and tossed it over the side of the boat.

Here's the Drill: D

Practice the D sound in words that begin with *d*. Feel your tongue touch the gum ridge before you let the air out—and vibrate those vocal cords!

drama	delicate
date	dream
dial	domain
drool	dollar
diaper	daybreak

Practice the D sound at the end of these words. Note that when the sound is in this final position, it is not necessary to expel as much air.

should	learned
valid	marinade
errand	marigold
road	arrived
board	scold

Practice the D sound in the middle of words. You will feel your tongue move to the gum ridge before the sound is spoken.

caddy	ruddy
puddle	ardor
radar	undeserving
addition	blunder
noodle	wonder

Advanced Practice

Now's the time to show off your skills by using the correctly produced D sounds in sentences. Use proper American intonation when you read the sentences.

1. Darwin's dog digs diligently in the dirt.

2. I don't think Debbie is delusional, do you?

3. It's dangerous to drink and drive on a dark road.

4. Darlene delivered the folder with my data inside.

5. The dinner was delicious, and dessert was delightful.

6. The dolphin dipped, flipped, waved, and then smiled!

7. Dad discovered my diary but said he didn't read it.

8. We had a delicious dinner of dietary delights.

9. Brad has lived in Denmark, Dublin, Denver, and Canada.

10. Dairy Queen is my favorite dessert destination.

Cough It Up! K and G

Phonetic Symbols: /k/ and /g/

The K and G sounds are plosive sounds because they start with a buildup and release. Unlike the P, B, T, and D sounds, however, these two sounds take shape in a different position. The previous plosives we discussed were formed in the front of your mouth. Now we're moving back, about as far back in your mouth as you can go. If you stretch your tongue back far enough you can feel your soft palate. That's where the action will take place. If you're not sure where we are, make a little cough and you'll feel movement in the part of the inside of your mouth that we're talking about.

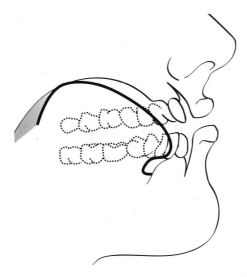

The back of the tongue touches the soft palate for both the K and G sounds.

How You Do It

Form the K sound by raising the back of your tongue to touch the soft palate. Air is then built up and released through the mouth. The G sound follows the same pattern, but is voiced.

Common Mistakes

Although accented speakers usually do not have much difficulty producing these sounds, there is sometimes a tendency to substitute K for G. In other words, you need to be sure that your vocal cords are vibrating when you're making the G sound.

Listening Practice

 Track 18: To hear the difference between the K and G sounds, listen to the CD.

Beginning:	cool	crazy	customer	kitchen
Middle:	walking	local	picture	risky
End:	quick	take	bank	truck

Beginning:	good	game	goal	guess
Middle:	legal	bagpipe	forget	begin
End:	egg	drag	league	snag

Here's the Drill: K

You will get a good feel for the pressure building up behind your tongue when you practice the K sound at the beginning of words. Note that the letters *k*, *c*, *ch*, and *q* all stand for the K sound in the initial position in these words. Repeat the list several times.

kitchen	chorus
crate	cough
crazy	caffeine
quiz	Kathleen
customer	combat

Make sure that the voiceless K can be heard at the end of words. Stress it more than you have to at first, then try it in a more natural style. Again, you will notice that *c*, *k*, *ck*, and *q* represent the K sound in the final position in these words.

quack	Iraq
antique	Barack
bank	cloak
sack	bleak
zodiac	click

Practice the K sound in the middle of words. Feel the connection between your soft palate and tongue in the middle position.

murky	liquor
pickle	doctor
inquire	oculist
macadamia	Chicago
ruckus	escapade

Advanced Practice

Make up your own sentences, or use mine. The goal is to use the correct K sound in as natural a way as possible while also using correct intonation. Remember to rise in pitch on key words. Because different letters represent the K sound, you might want to underline those letters in these sentences.

1. The kitchen curtains looked quite clean.

2. The customer asked for antique moccasins.

3. The truck drove into Quick Lube on the weekend.

4. I had a quiet breakfast before calling the bank.

5. Kate was walking quickly down the sidewalk.

6. Mack got in an accident around two o'clock.

7. What is the cost of the shack near the creek?

8. Could you take my ticket and inquire about a replacement?

9. The carnival was selling pink cotton candy.

10. Can I ask you a quick question about this artwork?

Here's the Drill: G

Using the correct sound in the initial position of words is pretty easy. It'll give you confidence to try the G sound when it occurs in other positions in words. Just remember, this is a voiced sound; do not confuse it with the K sound.

ghost	garden
gallop	goal
graveyard	goodness
green	group
gasoline	goose

You're doing great. Now, practice these words that end with the G sound. Make up some sentences of your own with these words for extra practice.

catalog	vague
frog	wig
egg	jog
league	brag
fatigue	clog

Now the G is in the middle of the word. Don't over-punch it. Give it the same energy as the other sounds in the words.

bagpipe	bigger
magazine	regal
forget	stagger
hungry	sugar
bagel	ago

Advanced Practice

Now you can practice the G sound with the principles of American intonation. Raise your pitch on the key words and remember to make the voiced G sound, not the voiceless K sound.

1. I caught a glimpse of a ghost behind the graveyard.
2. I got a magazine at the grocery store.
3. The catalog was filled with gear and gizmos.
4. Garth is so hungry he could eat a goose.
5. A green frog was in my garden.
6. Isn't it great how much Gwen has grown?
7. I asked for a bagel and got a beagle instead.
8. The tour guide plagued us with the bagpipes.
9. I went to Grand Rapids and then to the Gulf of Mexico.
10. The price of gasoline is going up again.

The Least You Need to Know

♦ Plosives are consonant sounds that we form by first building up pressure and then releasing it.

♦ For the P and B sounds, expel air from between the lips.

◆ To form the T and D sounds, release pressure from the gum ridge behind the upper teeth.

◆ The K and G sounds rely on the back of the tongue and the soft palate to produce their unique sounds.

Chapter 11

Going With the Flow

In This Chapter

- ♦ Why creating friction can be a good thing
- ♦ How hearing difficult sounds makes pronunciation easier
- ♦ Which tricky spellings can cause confusion

Get ready to meet the *fricative* family. That's a word that linguists use to define sounds that have certain things in common. The fricatives start out as all other sounds until an articulator gets in the way and changes the shape or flow of things. But it's not an unwelcome intrusion. It's just a way to create the unique character of each sound.

By the way, you already learned about several fricatives. Voiceless th, voiced TH, and the S and Z sounds needed some extra attention, so we put those in Chapters 8 and 9.

Create Some Friction: F and V

Phonetic Symbols: /f/ and /v/

The key factor in fricative sounds is that they all have a continuous flow. So regardless of where your articulators are during the production of the sound, you should be able to continue the flow of the sound until you run out of breath.

How You Do It

To create the proper F sound, place the upper teeth over your lower lip and let the air flow. It's that simple. If your intention is to create a V sound, just duplicate that action but make sure your vocal cords are vibrating.

For both F and V, the upper teeth come in direct contact with the lower lip.

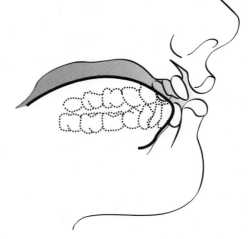

Common Mistakes

Be careful about the amount of contact between your lip and teeth. Relax and let things happen naturally. The pressure can't be too forceful. On the other hand, if there's not enough pressure, your sound will be inaudible.

There's another error some accented speakers make. Instead of making the F sound, they make a B sound or sometimes a W sound. In both cases, the speakers fail to put the upper teeth and lower lip in contact.

Listening Practice

Track 19: Listen to the CD as I demonstrate both F and V sounds in words. Repeat after me and feel what your teeth and lips are doing!

Beginning:	fine	fan	phone	full
Middle:	effect	laughter	defend	before
End:	safe	knife	half	giraffe

Beginning:	vast	vine	vapor	victory
Middle:	favor	never	moving	cover
End:	prove	cave	dive	love

Here's the Drill: F

Now read the following list of words that begin with the F sound. When you practice, exaggerate the sound during your first reading and then gradually reduce the sound to a natural level of intensity.

field	fiasco
foreign	far
fragile	feeble
football	photo
ferment	foolish

When the F sound is at the end of a word, make sure it is as audible as the other sounds. When practicing, you may want to give it a little more intensity than you normally would. But eventually, you need to produce the F sound at the same level as you do the other sounds.

safe	half
giraffe	staff
grief	relief
laugh	beef
wife	belief

The following words contain the F sound in its most difficult position. If you are still having problems, try the previous lists again and then come back when you're ready.

coffee	affiliate
mafia	caffeine
laughter	cafeteria
coughed	goofy
symphony	driftwood

Advanced Practice

If it will help you, underline the letters in each word that represent the F sound. Remember that F is not the only letter that makes that particular sound, so don't rely on spelling. By the way, don't just read the sentence, use proper intonation and say it like you mean it!

1. Stephanie left her phone at the philharmonic.

2. My friends laughed when the giraffe ate the taffy.

3. The staff at the symphony was professional and friendly.

4. The fox followed Felix the ferret into the forest.

5. Felicia and Freddy found five fireflies with a flashlight.

6. Freddie ate four foot-long hotdogs and doesn't feel well.

7. The professor focused on foreign affairs on Friday.

8. It's really laughable what some folks call fashion.

9. My friend Felicity said she found the meaning of life.

10. He fractured his foot while trying to find the phone.

Here's the Drill: V

Read the following list of words that contain the V sound in the initial position. Exaggerate the sound more than you normally would at first, then gradually work your way toward a more normal sound. Be careful not to substitute a B or W sound!

veal	veil
very	victim
vacation	vest
Venice	victory
vocal	volume

So far you are doing great! In the words in the next list, the V sound is the last sound you hear. Be careful not to give it too much force when you say it.

glove	hive
five	love
olive	cave
alive	brave
believe	shove

When you feel ready, test your new skill by saying the words in the next list; they have the V sound in the middle position. If it's too difficult at first, try the sound at the end of words and come back. Just take your time. Eventually it will seem as if you've been doing it all your life.

gravy	savor
division	flavor
Bavaria	endeavor
movie	livid
travel	pivot

Advanced Practice

Now is the time to show off what you have learned. In the sentences that follow, the V sound can be found in all positions of words. When you first read the sentences, concentrate on pronunciation. Then read them again and deliver them in a conversational style—along with correct pronunciation, of course.

1. Victor voraciously ate the veal that was to serve everyone.

2. The voice box vibrates for certain consonants and all vowels.

3. Veronica traveled to Venice with her golden retriever.

4. Do me a favor and let me have seventy dollars?

5. Prove to me that you love me as much as you loved Victoria.

6. Steve will be serving caviar and veal chops.

7. The vice president voiced his opposition to the veto.

8. She plans to travel to Bavaria, Vienna, and Czechoslovakia.

9. The movie was too violent for a love story.

10. There's a flight to Kiev that leaves in fifty-five minutes.

Smooth and Silky Sounds: SH and ZH

Phonetic Symbols: /ʃ/ and /ʒ/

These two sounds are also members of the fricative family because each has a continuous flow. As long as you can provide the air, these sounds will continue. The SH sound is second nature to parents, teachers, and librarians because it is the universal sound for, "Be quiet!" The ZH sound is a bit less familiar to many because it has French overtones. You'll see what I mean as we go along.

How You Do It

For SH, the tip of your tongue is close to your upper gum line but it does not touch it. The sides of your tongue come in contact with your upper molars and your breath stream flows down the center of your tongue. Make sure your lips are slightly rounded.

The mate to SH is ZH. As with previous pairs of sounds, the only difference is the vibration of the vocal cords. In this case, SH is the voiceless sound, and ZH is the voiced sound. The ZH sound is unusual because it almost sounds more French than English. In fact, the ZH sound *is* very common in French.

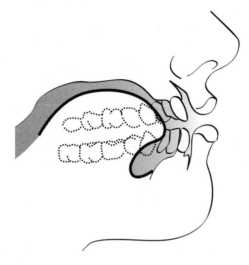

For the SH and ZH sounds, air flows down the center of your tongue, and the lips are slightly rounded.

Common Mistakes

Some non-native English speakers substitute CH for SH. For example, they might say "choose" when they meant to say "shoes." Or they may describe wooly animals as "cheep" instead of "sheep." The difference between the sounds is that the tip of the tongue contacts the gum line for the CH sound, but it should not contact the gum line—or anywhere else—for the SH sound.

Another common error that some people make is to produce an S or Z sound instead of SH or ZH. In Chapter 9 I talked about the S and Z. If you need additional practice, re-visit that chapter. You need to be able to hear distinct differences between all sounds to be successful in minimizing your accent.

Listening Practice

Track 20: The SH and ZH sounds can be tricky. Listen carefully to how I pronounce them on the CD. Note that the ZH sound rarely occurs in the beginning of English words.

Beginning:	show	shower	should	shall
Middle:	motion	function	usher	Russia
End:	dish	push	crash	brush

Beginning:	Jacques			
Middle:	pleasure	leisure	usual	casual
End:	rouge	garage	beige	collage

Here's the Drill: SH

When you first practice the SH sound, give it a little extra punch at the beginning of a word. Really listen to it. After you get a feel for the proper way of pronouncing it and it starts to feel natural, decrease the intensity and practice it in a normal tone.

shoe	sheep
shine	ship
shell	show
shape	shallow
shark	share

Producing the SH sound at the end of a word will give you necessary practice in shifting from different sounds to the SH. If you have conquered the first list, this one should be a breeze!

flash	rash
lash	rush
bush	brush
fish	splash
crash	crush

Other letters, besides *sh*, may also stand for the SH sound in the middle of a word. One that occurs frequently is the *tion* ending, which is pronounced "shun." Other letters and combinations that stand for the SH sound include *c* and *ss*. As you practice the following words, make note of their spelling.

mission	fishing
wished	mashed
cashed	subtraction
ocean	delicious
ratio	mushroom

Advanced Practice

Now's your chance to use proper American intonation while practicing the SH sound. First, read the sentences to get a feel for proper pronunciation. Then look away from the page and pretend you're using these sentences in a real conversation.

1. Michelle ordered fish and mashed potatoes.

2. I shouldn't have paid cash for the mansion.

3. She sells seashells by the seashore.

4. Your shoes are so shiny and fashionable.

5. The ship sailed over the ocean and then washed ashore.

6. Put some lotion on your rash and then wash it off.

7. I wish I didn't have to share this shrimp with Shirley.

8. Sharon took her share of cash and shopped for dishes.

9. She shoved Sean into the bush before she bashed him.

10. We collected shark teeth in the shallows near the shore.

Here's the Drill: ZH

Do you notice anything unusual about the list that follows? There really aren't many words in American English that begin with the ZH sound. Notice the different letters that represent the ZH sound.

Jacques	genre

As you develop a better feel for how ZH occurs in words, continue to practice its proper pronunciation. Don't work too hard to force this sound at the end of a word. It's a very smooth sound with little facial tension.

camouflage	beige
decoupage	sabotage
concierge	Bruges
garage	rouge
triage	corsage

When the ZH sound occurs in the middle of a word, there are a number of letters and letter combinations that might stand for the sound. You'll notice the variety in the following list. Notice that the ZH sound is never represented by *zh*.

I suggest that you first read the following list out loud and make special note of the spellings. Do this several times and try to develop a feel for the different letters that represent the ZH sound.

casual	Persian
treasure	unusual
decision	leisure
seizure	television
cashmere	visual

Advanced Practice

Now that you have a better idea of which letters stand for the ZH sound, try incorporating what you have learned as you say the following sentences. As always, use American intonation with rises and falls in pitch.

1. He always wore a beige leisure suit.
2. The concierge said that it would be his pleasure to serve us.
3. Measure the ingredients or you'll sabotage the soufflé.
4. Jacques treasured the decoupage his children made.
5. The television show was about illegal search and seizure.
6. The sky was an unusual azure blue.
7. Look in the garage for your old camouflage gear.
8. This cashmere sweater feels so luscious.
9. The magician entertained us with visual illusions.
10. It was the teacher's decision to do long division.

Close to a Whisper: H

Phonetic Symbol: /h/

The H sound, if you think about it, is really a whisper. It is a difficult sound for non-native English speakers because it's hard to provide specific instructions on how to produce it. But with a combination of direction and listening, I'm certain you will soon be pronouncing it perfectly.

How You Do It

The H sound is produced far back in your throat and is made by exhaling through your mouth in a slightly audible manner. It's important that the sound be as smooth as possible with no roughness or throaty quality. It should simply sound like air.

The H is a smooth, airy sound produced far back in your throat.

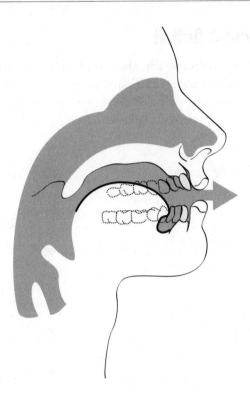

Common Mistakes

There are common substitutions that some people make for H. Instead of the airy, smooth quality, W, V, or a throaty R sound is used in its place.

Listening Practice

Track 21: Listen to how I pronounce the H sound on the CD. It's essentially a whisper. The H sound does not occur at the end of a word.

Beginning:	happy	habit	hedge	who
Middle:	inhale	behind	rehearse	behold

Here's the Drill: H

In some English words, the *h* is silent. This occurs most often at the beginning of a word. Although silent *h* is an infrequent occurrence, producing an H when it shouldn't be there will call attention to accented speech. The best way to find out for sure about the pronunciation is with a dictionary.

Following are some words whose initial *h* is silent in American English.

honor	hour
herbal	heir

Practice the H sound at the beginning of the following words. Repeat them until you are comfortable with the sound.

hello	hold
help	helpless
Halloween	Halifax
hungry	hippo
humble	harbor

The H sound does not occur in the final position in American English. In the list that follows, you'll find the H sound in the middle of each word. Remember that the sound needs to be audible, but really has no sound of its own.

bohemian	behave
somehow	cohabitation
cohort	rehearse
exhale	Baja
Manhattan	unheard

Advanced Practice

When you become tired of practicing these sentences, develop a few of your own. Add words that are relevant to your job and your life so they become more meaningful to you when you use American intonation.

1. It's horrible what the haze and humidity do to my hair.
2. Helen and Harry dressed as a hippopotamus for Halloween.
3. She is hungry, dehydrated, and unhealthy.
4. The hot air balloon was high over Manhattan.
5. Cohabitation was unheard of in my day.
6. In my humble opinion, Harriet hindered the rehearsal.
7. Harry said my Mohawk hairstyle was too Bohemian.
8. Even though he looked like a hunk, he didn't behave like a human.
9. Sahara said it's hopeless; her heart belongs to Harry.
10. His cohort works for a hedge fund in Valhalla.

The Least You Need to Know

- Remember not to rely on spelling. It's the sound that matters.
- When producing the V sound, don't make the common mistake of substituting B for V.
- Even though a sound may be voiceless, it still must be heard. Don't drop any sounds, especially the final sound of a word.

Chapter

Sounds in a Category by Themselves

In This Chapter

- ◆ Discover unique "stop and go" sounds
- ◆ Learn how two sounds combine to make one
- ◆ Find out how to incorporate these into your everyday speech

Stop and go sounds? What are those all about? It sounds as though we need to incorporate a traffic signal into your practice routine. But these sounds are not as complicated as you might think. It simply means that you will take sounds that we have already discussed and join them. But before you deliver these sounds, you need to stop and think. That's valuable advice in many arenas.

Stop and Go: CH and DJ

Phonetic Symbols: /tʃ/ and /dʒ/

The CH and DJ sounds are close cousins to the fricative family. Even though they share a common trait, they also have unique characteristics, which is why linguists have a name for them—*affricatives*. This bit of information may help if you are having difficulty substituting one of the continually flowing sounds (fricatives) with the stop and go of CH or DJ.

How You Do It

It may help you to think of forming the voiceless CH sound as a two-step process—a combination of T and SH. First, place the tip of your tongue on your gum line as if you're ready to make the T sound. After air pressure builds up, send out a quick burst of air, quickly moving to the SH sound.

The voiced DJ sound is usually represented by the letter *j*. To produce it, place the tip of your tongue on your gum line as if you're ready to make the D sound. After pressure builds up, quickly move into the ZH sound.

The CH sound is made by combining the T and SH sounds, and the DJ sound is made by combining the D and ZH sounds.

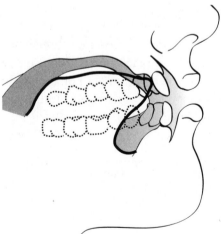

Common Mistakes

The most common habit accented speakers have is to substitute the SH and ZH sounds for the CH and DJ sounds. To correct this error, make sure you place your tongue tip on your gum ridge prior to releasing a burst of air.

Listening Practice

Track 22: Listen carefully to the CH and DJ sounds on the CD. It will make pronouncing them easier. Repeat after me!

Beginning:	chair	chew	champion	check
Middle:	butcher	marching	patched	catcher
End:	watch	lunch	batch	coach

Beginning:	joke	Japan	jury	junk
Middle:	wages	engaged	majesty	pageant
End:	fudge	marriage	cage	wedge

Here's the Drill: CH

Prior to producing each word, make sure the tip of your tongue is on the upper gum line as though you are starting to produce the T sound. Continue to practice this list of words until you can hear the difference between CH and SH and can correctly articulate both sounds. When producing the CH sound, it may help to think of a child's imitation of a train—choo-choo!

chug	chuckle
chips	chick
chilly	choke
Chinese	checkers
chicken	Charleston

Keep in mind that a burst of air will occur at the end of each of the following words. Again, start with T in mind and move from there.

birch	witch
each	patch
match	thatch
Dutch	crutch
beach	batch

Try the CH sound in the middle of these words. Take your time. It can be tricky at first.

catcher	bunches
marching	maturity
poached	butchered
roaches	enriching
watched	hatchet

Advanced Practice

Let's see how well you have learned this lesson. It may make practicing easier to underline the letters that represent the CH sound.

1. Charlie got a chuckle when she saw the chicks hatching.

2. It was surely a challenge to cook fried chicken.

3. Rachel had a grilled cheese sandwich and chocolate shake.

4. Chuck had to wear crutches after he challenged Mitch.

5. The Chinese restaurant had chop suey and fortune cookies.

6. Challenge the champion to a re-match!

7. The coach was chatting with the catcher about the match.

8. Butch said the teacher chose some chips for lunch.

9. Rachel said there was a chill in the air after church.

10. How much wood did that cheery woodchuck chop?

Here's the Drill: DJ

Remember that the DJ sound is the voiced version of the CH sound. Begin by getting ready to make the voiced D and then give a quick burst of air, with your vocal cords vibrating, to produce the ZH sound. It sounds more complicated than it is. Try it in the beginning of these words.

jealous	jest
jeopardy	justice
January	Jeep
jelly	Germany
Japan	jaws

The DJ sound at the end of words is also a voiced sound, of course. Keep in mind that your vocal cords need to vibrate and the sound needs to be audible.

marriage	lodge
enrage	badge
fudge	sludge
wedge	usage
large	page

The DJ sound is more difficult in the middle of a word. Practice each one slowly until it feels comfortable. Don't get discouraged!

sergeant	enraged
margarine	pages
allegiance	hedges
pageant	ledger
magician	hedgehog

Advanced Practice

Put it all together and test your newly learned skill in a sentence format. After reading each sentence several times for practice, pretend they are part of a conversation and say them with meaning, using the rules of American intonation.

1. Joey and Madge pledged their allegiance to the flag.

2. The sergeant told the major that Germany had lost the war.

3. Madge refused to budge until she finished all her fudge.

4. The judge admonished the jury for joking.

5. I plan to go to Japan in June and July.

6. We can't use a carriage for our marriage if it's in January.

7. Georgette nudged Virginia and said she was on the wrong page.

8. When Janie heard the joke, she was enraged!

9. I always put margarine and jam or jelly on my toast.

10. Marjorie thought the pageant judges made the wrong decision.

The Least You Need to Know

♦ The CH sound is a perfect combination of the T and SH sounds.

♦ The DJ sound combines D with ZH as smoothly as possible.

♦ Hearing a sound produced correctly on a regular basis might work better for you than trying to read the instructions.

Chapter 13

Making Nice with Nasals

In This Chapter

- ◆ Meet the nasal trio: M, N, NG
- ◆ The critical role of the soft palate
- ◆ Avoiding the mistakes of many Americans

It could be that we take our noses for granted. Yes, everyone is concerned about its size and how it looks on his or her face, but when you think about it, it really is a truly remarkable instrument. Not only does it help us with our sense of smell and breathing, but it helps give our voices a unique quality called nasality.

Your Lips Are Sealed: M

Phonetic Symbol: /m/

I don't think I need to go into very much detail about producing the M sound, at least from the perspective of your lips. If you can keep your lips together and direct the air into your nasal passage, you can successfully make this sound. It's called humming.

To produce the M sound, your lips are together and the soft palate is lowered.

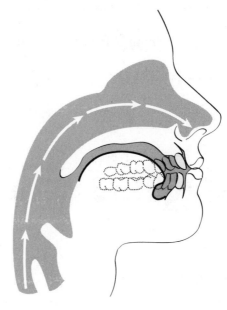

How You Do It

The sound is made by gently closing the lips, dropping the soft palate, and using your vocal cords. Because your soft palate is open, the air goes into your nose. The M is a long sound and you sustain it.

Common Mistakes

Some languages have a greater degree of nasality than American English. But most languages do include nasality. So, you are likely to be accustomed to the sound itself, but the level of nasality may differ from the standard American intonation. See Appendix C to see if nasality may be an issue for you.

Listening Practice

Track 23: You probably won't have too much trouble with the M sound. But try a little listening practice just in case.

Beginning:	me	mother	maid	marriage
Middle:	comma	famous	glamour	drama
End:	aim	farm	jam	drum

Here's the Drill: M

You shouldn't have any trouble producing the sound itself. Think more about your voice quality. Gently squeeze your nose and you should feel it vibrating slightly when saying the initial sounds of the words in this list.

middle	most
milk	machine
motel	macaroni
mister	mustard
moist	million

The last sound in each of the following words requires that air flow through the nose. Again, the soft palate is lowered so air can travel through the nose.

dorm	storm
alarm	plumb
film	auditorium
mushroom	rhyme
room	dream

Remember to think "American voice quality" when you are making the M sound in the middle of words.

common	formula
limit	feminine
camera	army
laminate	dermatologist
vermin	sermon

Advanced Practice

See how well you do with the M sounds in sentences. Remember your intonation and pitch. Start slowly and build up to a more natural rate of speech.

1. Mary was dismayed when the alarm sounded in her dorm.

2. The managers met in the auditorium to see the film.

3. Make mine with extra mushrooms, mustard, and mayonnaise.

4. Mother made Dad go to the market in the middle of the night.

5. Michael was manager of a motel with bad plumbing.

6. Amanda made lemon meringue pie for her Mom.

7. Millions of men and women meet one another on e-Harmony.

8. Maurice measured the miles between Minnesota and Michigan.

9. The plumber managed to find time to fix the bathroom sink.

10. The mayor and minister made some opening remarks.

Very "N"-teresting: N

Phonetic Symbol: /n/

This sound could be a tricky one, especially for Asian speakers because they often have difficulty hearing the sound. Spend time reading this material and underline words that have the N sound in them before you start practicing.

How You Do It

The N sound is made with the tip of the tongue placed lightly yet firmly against the tooth ridge. Once again, the tongue is not touching the teeth. N is a nasal sound, which means that the soft palate is lowered so the air can go into the nose. The position of the tongue for N is similar to T. The tongue must be completely relaxed, filling the entire mouth and touching the insides of all the teeth, leaving no room for the air to go except through the nose.

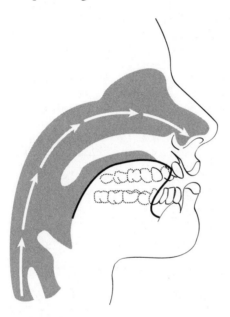

The N requires a firm yet light touch of the tongue to the tooth ridge.

Common Mistakes

A common mistake among Asian speakers is substituting the L sound in place of N. Both sounds have a similar tongue placement—with the tongue on the tooth ridge—but with N the air exits through the nose. L is not a nasal sound.

To test yourself, see if you can feel the vibration where your tongue tip touches the tooth ridge behind the upper front teeth. Notice that you can sustain the N sound. It is a long sound, not a quick one.

Listening Practice

Track 24: Listen as I produce the N sound in all word positions. The tip of the tongue is placed lightly yet firmly against the ridge behind your teeth. The N sound is a nasal one, which means that the soft palate is lowered so air can go into the nose.

Beginning:	nasal	never	nice	nature
Middle:	connect	Santa	canopy	funny
End:	brain	earn	heaven	rain

Here's the Drill: N

Practice the sound on its own before starting in on this list. Make sure you are saying N and are not substituting another sound.

navigate	newspaper
nature	necessity
nasty	knowledge
noodle	notes
knuckle	never

Producing the N sound at the end of words should be easy for you if you have the correct tongue placement and your soft palate is lowered.

queen	fascination
bone	obsession
mission	incarceration
fashion	shin
education	sunshine

Test yourself with N in the middle of words. If it's difficult, refer to the soft palate exercises in Chapter 5.

handle	danger
finally	candor
winter	Cinderella
sunnier	contrary
Indiana	answer

Sentence Practice

If you need to have less nasality in your speech, work on lifting your soft palate. That, along with proper pitch and intonation, will result in less accented speech. Keep the feeling of a slight yawn.

1. Noisy Nora nibbles on nutritious nuts.

2. Never mind that noise, you need to pay attention!

3. It was nice of Ned to notice my new mittens.

4. Nicholas lost a nickel near the pond.

5. Nancy had no idea that Nora was so sensitive.

6. Never underestimate feminine intuition.

7. We lived in Kinsale, Ireland, and took the train to Dublin.

8. Henry spent a fortune on his new fur-lined moccasins.

9. We went downtown to have lunch and to try on the new fashions.

10. He went to Washington to see the monuments.

We Go Back a Long Way: NG

Phonetic Symbol: /ŋ/

The NG sound is very common in American English, especially because so many words end in "ing." It's a sound that Americans very often mispronounce.

How You Do It

The NG is a voiced nasal sound. You have to go way back in your mouth to produce it correctly. The back of your tongue must have a strong contact with your soft palate to seal it off and produce the nasal sound that is required.

Notice how the back of the tongue is in contact with the soft palate for the NG sound.

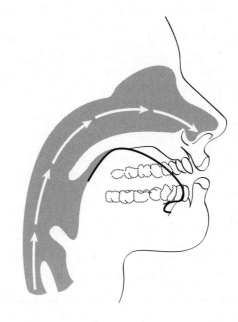

Common Mistakes

Many people eliminate the final *g* when a word ends in "ing." So, for example, instead of "sitting" and "looking," they say "sittin" and "lookin." Although many Americans do this in casual conversation, I recommend that you pronounce the "ing" combination properly, as NG.

Another habit is to substitute a voiceless K for the voiced G. For example, "runnink" instead of "running" and "thinkink" instead of "thinking."

Some non-native English speakers add an extra syllable to a word that ends in G. It may be the result of putting too much punch or pressure on the final sound. Example: "fishing-uh" or "swing-uh."

When "ing" is followed by another "ing," a common error is to voice the *g* at the end of the first "ing." Example: "sing-ging" instead of "singing" or "ring-ging" instead of "ringing."

Listening Practice

Track 25: Listen to the words with the NG sound. The back of my tongue will have strong contact with my soft palate to seal it off and produce the nasal sound that is required. Repeat after me. By the way, there are no American English words that begin with the NG sound.

Middle:	anger	ringing	stinging	linger
End:	long	Hong Kong	sang	wing

Here's the Drill: NG

Notice that there are no NG sounds at the beginning of American English words. Let's start with NG at the end of words.

song	bang
strong	gong
belong	ding
ring	filming
going	swimming

It's a bit trickier to produce the NG sound in the middle of words. Be careful that you do not substitute the K sound for NG. Also do not voice a *g* when it's followed by "ing." However, when the NG sound is followed by letter combinations other than "ing," we do voice the *g*, as in *finger*. There are some exceptions, but keeping the general rule in mind will serve our purposes.

finger	winging
angry	banging
linger	longer
tingle	tangle
wrangler	thronging

Advanced Practice

Put all your new skills to the test and try these sentences, first by reading them aloud and then in a natural conversational tone.

1. I was going to play Ping-Pong.

2. Though she felt cranky, Mary went hiking.

3. He was born in Reading, Pennsylvania.

4. Walking or climbing is great exercise.

5. Is Barry going to sing us a song?

6. He was pointing his finger at me!

7. Ling-Ling has been gone a long time.

8. Ding, dong the witch is dead!

9. The bird was attempting to fly with one wing.

10. Sing-Sing prison is in Ossining, New York.

The Least You Need to Know

◆ When you speak most sounds, the soft palate lifts and closes off the nasal passage.

◆ When you make nasal sounds, the soft palate lowers and the air comes through the nose.

◆ Even though many Americans drop the final *g* in words ending in "ing," you will sound more professional if you pronounce the complete NG sound.

◆ To see if you have the correct degree of nasality, pinch the openings of your nose and try to hum. If you can't, you're doing it correctly.

Chapter  14

A Smooth Ride with the Glides

In This Chapter

- ♦ How a consonant can be bullied by a vowel
- ♦ Why whistling may prove to be an essential skill
- ♦ How to avoid common sound substitutions

My guess is that you're not that interested in how consonants are categorized. So although you probably won't ever bring this up during dinner conversation, defining the consonants and their common characteristics is important because it makes the learning process easier. Trust me. In this chapter, we talk about glides, or semi-vowels. These are voiced sounds that are made with a gliding movement and they give a shape to your mouth that is similar to a vowel. By the way, if you are looking for R and L in this category, review Chapter 8 where more time is spent on the more troublesome sounds.

The Wild, Wild W

Phonetic Symbol: /w/

In this section, let's discuss *w*. There's no doubt that it's a sound that occurs frequently in American English, so it's something you need to perfect. But there's controversy over a similar sound—the WH sound. Many linguists feel it isn't a sound that's used anymore; most people pronounce it as the W sound. For that reason, we'll skip over the WH for now. But if you're a purist and want to learn it, just add a little voiceless whoosh before you make the W sound. I'll demonstrate it for you a little later on the CD.

How You Do It

The W sound is produced by tensing and puckering your lips as if you're whistling. The tip of your tongue is pointing down and your vocal cords are vibrating. You can feel the vibration on your lips.

To produce the W sound, your tongue tip is down, your lips are slightly puckered, and your vocal cords vibrate.

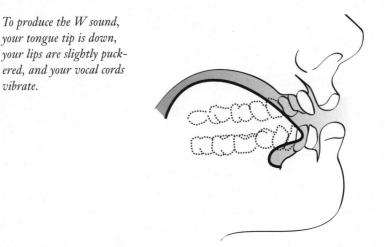

Common Mistakes

If there is an error for this sound, it's that some people substitute the V sound for W. If you find yourself in the habit, take some time and revisit Chapter 10 and see how the V is made. Basically, your top teeth are on your lower lip and your vocal cords are vibrating. As you have seen in the illustration, the teeth are not involved when making the W sound.

Listening Practice

Track 26: Time for some listening practice! Note that though the letter *w* does appear at the end of English words, it does not make the W sound in that position.

Beginning:	wonder	wizard	winter	Wyoming
Middle:	mower	chowder	shower	plowing

Here's the Drill: W

Remember to pucker your lips slightly as you produce the W sound at the beginning of words. If you feel your lower teeth touching your upper lip, you are making it incorrectly.

work	weapon
want	weasel
will	wonderful
witness	whiskers
walk	window

The situation changes when *w* is in the middle of a word because it may take on characteristics of the adjoining vowel sound.

coward	growling
powder	slower
rowdy	powerful
louder	mower
flowers	rowing

Advanced Practice

When *w* occurs at the end of a word, it is usually pronounced as a diphthong—a double vowel sound. (For example: *cow* ends with an

OW diphthong.) You'll learn more about diphthongs in the next chapter. For now, try these sentences jam-packed with the W sound.

1. The warden watched the rowdy workers from his tower.
2. The waiter was wondering how much Walter would order.
3. Wilma wanted nothing to do with the cowboy.
4. My wife put laundry detergent in the dishwasher and broke it.
5. The witness swore loudly that Willy Wonka was innocent.
6. They issued a warrant after they found the weapon.
7. The powerful wind whipped the flowers out of the ground.
8. Willy the wild wolf went west for the winter.
9. Walter Whipple warned the weary warrior.
10. Wally wanted to know whether the warden was aware of the waste.

Why the Worry: Y

Phonetic Symbol: /j/

Don't let the phonetic symbol confuse you. We're going to work on the Y sound in words such as *yellow* and *yo-yo*.

The Y sound calls for action in the middle and back of the tongue.

How You Do It

The Y sound is formed by raising the middle of the tongue up to the hard palate. Then the tongue immediately takes shape for the next vowel. Your vocal cords are vibrating.

Common Mistakes

The primary mistake that non-native speakers make is to substitute the J sound for the Y sound. For example, you may have heard non-native speakers saying "jello" when they mean "yellow." Some comedians imitate the sound substitution as part of a stereotypical "foreign" accent. If you're the target of the joke, I'm sure you'll fail to see the humor. It should only be short-lived, though. This substitution is easy to correct.

Listening Practice

Track 27: If you're having trouble with the Y sound, listening will help. Note that although the letter *y* often appears at the end of words, it is usually pronounced as EE when preceded by a consonant. For that reason, there are no words in the following list with the Y sound at the end.

Beginning:	yellow	yoga	yeast	yowl
Middle:	mayor	flying	player	crayon

Here's the Drill: Y

Practice the Y sound at the beginning of words. Keep in mind that the middle and back part of your tongue will be used. If you feel the tip of your tongue touch the gum ridge behind your upper teeth, you are making the sound incorrectly.

yellow	yard
yo-yo	yammer
yacht	yarn
yesterday	year
Yankees	yes

Now concentrate on practicing the Y sound in the middle of the following words.

destroyer	crying
lawyer	trying
mayo	paying
employer	fraying
foyer	staying

When you find the Y sound at the end of the word, it sounds more like a diphthong, a close combination of two vowels. For example, in the word *toy*, the *y* sounds like *oi*. We will address diphthongs in Part 4.

Advanced Practice

Remember that if the tip of your tongue is touching the palate or the gum ridge when making the Y sound, you are not making the sound correctly.

1. The boyish young man was a champion yo-yo player.

2. I heard Yo-Yo Ma in concert yesterday.

3. The lawyer yearned for mayo.

4. He was a player for the New York Yankees.

5. Her employer saw her yawn during yesterday's meeting.

6. Yolanda wanted the yak out of her yard.

7. She ate some yogurt before her yoga class.

8. The people on the yellow yacht are yelling to us.

9. Yum-Yum the Cat looked out at the yard, yearning to be free.

10. The lawyer is waiting in the foyer for you.

The Least You Need to Know

◆ Glides, also known as semi-vowels, are voiced sounds that are made with a gliding movement and that give a shape to your mouth that is similar to a vowel.

◆ Many people substitute the V sound for the W sound.

◆ A common error is to substitute the J sound for the Y sound.

Part 4

Pronunciation: Challenging Vowels and Diphthongs

Just as consonants pose problems for English language learners, vowels and diphthongs may cause difficulties as well. Diphthongs, by the way, are two vowels that glide from one to the other. As you can imagine, they can be tricky if you're not used to them.

There are many vowel sounds in American English with which you may be unfamiliar. Although there are just six letters of the alphabet that represent vowel sounds, there are more than 25 different sounds. But don't get discouraged. You probably need to work on only a few.

Conquering the vowels is important not only to reduce your accent, but to be understood. If you use an incorrect vowel, it could alter the meaning of an entire word. You'll be comforted to know that many people are having the same difficulty with certain vowels. For that reason, we'll tackle the most common problems first. Maybe all you need are a few minor adjustments!

Chapter 15

Victory Over Vowels

In This Chapter

- ◆ Learning the importance of vowels
- ◆ Discovering why vowels can be troublesome
- ◆ Finding out how subtle changes can create large problems

You have come upon an important chapter. Although vowels can be troublesome, you just can't have a word without one. In fact, you can't even have a syllable without one. Vowels give English words shape and specific meaning. That means that if even one vowel is mispronounced, it's going to have an impact on the entire word. If two vowels are mispronounced, your accent will stand out more than ever. As you know, most consonant difficulties that English language learners meet exist because the troublesome consonant sounds are not part of the person's first language. The same is true with vowels. No, I'm not saying that your native language doesn't have vowels. It's just that some are pronounced differently from the way American English vowels are pronounced. And one or two might be a new sound experience altogether.

All About Vowels

Now that you know how important vowels are, let's see exactly what a vowel is. A vowel is a sound that connects consonants to create words. A vowel is an open sound. Nothing gets in the way of the air stream when you produce a vowel. Vowels are made by slight changes in the position of the tongue and lips and by tensing or relaxing the muscles of your mouth. By prolonging or lengthening some vowel sounds, many words will sound more American. Perhaps the single most important factor in modifying vowel sounds is your ability to hear the sounds correctly. And because the differences between many vowels are subtle, that may not always be easy.

Vowels are always voiced; the vocal cords always vibrate in the production of a vowel. Vowels vary in length. A vowel in a stressed syllable lasts longer than the vowel in an unstressed syllable. In the word *finish*, for example, the *i* in the first syllable is given more importance than the unstressed *i* in the second syllable.

Linguists often refer to vowels according to classification. There are three vowel groups—front, center, and back—all of which refer to where the sound is produced in your mouth.

Short and Long Vowels

Track 28: One way of classifying vowels is by determining whether they represent a long sound or a short sound. You will hear on the CD not only the sound differences between long and short vowels but the way long vowels have more length or duration than short vowels. They're stretched out a little longer. Because this concept is important and often causes mispronunciations, take a look at the following lists of words that contain long and short vowel sounds. You will always know how to pronounce a long vowel—just say its letter.

The Long Vowel Sounds	The Short Vowel Sounds
a as in *acorn*	a as in *apple*
e as in *Easter*	e as in *let*
i as in *island*	i as in *pig*
o as in *open*	ah as in *hot*
u as in *universe*	uh as in *up*

The Rules of Long and Short

It's one thing to know what the short and long vowel sounds are. However, when you see a vowel in an unfamiliar word, how do you know how it's pronounced? Here are some rules that will help you to determine whether to pronounce a vowel as long or short:

1. Short vowels occur at the beginning or in the middle of words. When there is only one vowel in a word, the vowel usually stands for the short sound. Examples: *cat, hen, pill, pop, jump.*

2. When there are two vowels together in a word, the first vowel represents a long sound and the second vowel is silent. The phrase to remember is "When two vowels go walking, the first one does the talking." Examples: *boat, aim, beam.*

3. When the last vowel in a word is a silent *e*, the first vowel stands for a long vowel sound. Examples: *cake, Pete, bike, rope, tune.*

4. When the only vowel in a word comes at the end, it stands for a long sound. Examples: *hi, so, me, go, she, he.*

5. *Y* can sometimes act as a vowel. When it is the only vowel and it is at the end of a one-syllable word, it represents a long vowel sound. Examples: *my, by, sty.*

Of course, if you are really stuck, there's always the dictionary. As you know, I highly recommend having one handy not just for understanding vocabulary words but for pronunciation as well—especially if you know the International Phonetic Alphabet, which I discussed in Chapter 3.

Why Are Vowels So Difficult?

English vowel sounds are often difficult for non-native speakers to pronounce. One explanation is that there are five vowel letters in English (*a, e, i, o, u*—and sometimes *y*), but there are more than 25 vowel sounds. To make things even more complicated, there may be no clear relationship between the printed letter and its sound. Some vowel sounds have as many as 10 different spellings. Consider these words, for example: *cough, bough, dough, rough, through.* All have the same *ough* spelling, but there are five different pronunciations! Daunting, I know, but with practice, possible.

Another problem is the fact that some standard American English vowels don't occur in the speech patterns of any other language. As you would imagine, you need to do a considerable amount of active listening before you are able to pronounce and incorporate those sounds in your speech. But there is another big difference. Americans often do things bigger and bolder than people from other places—and speaking is one of those things. Americans aren't afraid to open their mouths to express themselves. But most non-native American English speakers aren't quite as flamboyant. The physical mouth openings for languages other than English are more conservative. Because several vowels require larger mouth openings, new English speakers need to get over feeling awkward if they want to pronounce the sounds American-style.

Most Common Problem Areas

There are three common mistakes of which non-native American English speakers should be aware:

1. Cutting a long vowel short.

    American speech has some long vowel sounds. I listed them earlier for you. It will take some practice to give the long sounds the duration that they require. The more you listen to American English, the more you will hear these long sounds that are so important to American speech. If you cut these sounds short, it will give your speech and intonation a choppy feel rather than the fluid motion that you want.

2. Substituting one vowel for another.

   If an American vowel does not exist in your first language, then your brain will substitute a sound that is totally different or make the best approximation. Again, as with the consonants, when a sound does not exist in your native language, your brain goes into default mode and substitutes a sound that is familiar. Unfortunately, the sound may not be close enough for an American listener to perceive as being correct. You may not hear the difference, but your American listener will. To get a better idea of the sounds that other languages have in common with English—and the sounds that differ from English—see Appendix C.

3. Producing a vowel with a rise in pitch.

   For many non-native American English speakers, it is a common habit to give an individual vowel a rise in pitch. All vowels must be produced on one level—flatly, with your voice in a monotone. If you hear your voice gliding upward when practicing vowel sounds, you are doing it incorrectly.

Don't Forget the Diphthongs

Don't panic about the diphthongs. They are simply two vowels that blend to form one vowel sound. Yes, it takes some acute listening skills and fast action on the part of the articulators, but with some tongue exercises and practice, you'll glide through them in no time. Chapter 18 deals with them in greater detail. It will give you something to look forward to! Plus it's the last chapter of the book!

The Least You Need to Know

- ◆ All American English words contain at least one vowel.
- ◆ There are 5 or 6 letters that represent vowel sounds, but more than 25 different sounds.
- ◆ There are many ways to classify vowels, but knowing whether a vowel sound is long or short is the most important.

◆ Be careful not to cut long vowels short or to substitute one vowel for another.

◆ When producing a vowel, keep your voice level to avoid a rise in pitch.

Chapter 16

Presenting the Front Vowels

In This Chapter

- ◆ Learning how a slip of the tongue could mean trouble
- ◆ Comparing vowel sounds that are similar but not the same
- ◆ Discovering vowels that are unique to English
- ◆ A few words about the central vowels

The front vowel is a type of vowel used in some spoken languages. Obviously, English is one of them. The defining characteristic of a front vowel is that the tongue is positioned as far forward as possible in the mouth without constricting the air stream.

The Vowel Is EE, as in EAT

Phonetic Symbol: /i/

The sound for EE is a long sound. It should not be a problem because it sounds just like the letter *e*.

How You Do It

The EE sound is produced with your mouth slightly open and lips spread as if you are smiling. The tip of your tongue touches the gum line behind your bottom teeth. It will help if you maintain some tension in the front of your tongue. Think of the letter *e* and stretch it out a bit.

Common Mistakes

Non-native speakers have a tendency to cut this vowel short. It is a long sound that is spoken in a monotone. Be careful not to let the pitch glide upward.

Word Practice

To help increase your awareness of the sound, when you practice the following words with the EE sound in the initial position, emphasize the sound a little more than you normally would. When you use it in actual speech, however, make sure that it receives the same emphasis as all the other sounds.

evening	easy
east	eagle
even	evil
Easter	eat

When the EE sound is at the end of a word, it is often spelled with the letter *y*. But, as you can see, this is not always the case. You need to be on your guard.

really	fancy
silly	she
family	funny
we	three

When the EE sound occurs in the middle of a word, you may have a tendency to cut the vowel short. Be careful to avoid this.

stream	freedom
cheese	trampoline
freeze	street
anyone	conceit

Advanced Practice

In the following sentences, all the occurrences of the EE sound are underlined to make practice easier. For a more difficult challenge, write your own sentences from the previous word lists.

1. The three boys had eaten all the cream cheese.
2. The comedy was really funny.
3. Louise and I went skiing last evening.
4. Mimi says that she's freezing.
5. The evil-looking eel was thirteen feet long.
6. Take it easy on the cookies, Howey.
7. Would you please read this story to me?
8. The movie was about evil and deceit.
9. The Jeep drove east toward Freedom Street.
10. Did you get a receipt for the pepperoni pizza?

The Vowel Is IH, as in IT

Phonetic Symbol: /ɪ/

The IH sound is produced a little lower in your mouth than the two previous vowels. It is a short vowel and is a new sound for many non-native English speakers.

How You Do It

The IH sound is produced by lowering and relaxing the tongue a bit. Your mouth is slightly open and your lips are slightly spread. It is a short vowel and should not be drawn out. There should be no rise in pitch.

Common Mistakes

Because this could be a new sound for you, take extra care. Although your lips are in a very slight smiling position, if you spread your lips too wide, it will sound like EE. This is, in fact, a common error that speakers make. Remember that EE is long and IH is short. Don't say "peeg" for *pig* or "meester" for *mister.* In fact, if you use the wrong vowel, it can change the entire meaning of a word. For example, *fit* can become *feet* and *mitt* can become *meat.* Check out the front vowel comparisons later in this chapter to help you distinguish the subtle differences among the sounds.

Word Practice

Remember that this vowel sound is a short sound. Don't substitute the long EE for this little quickie!

it	institute
inside	isn't
individual	if
important	Indian

Relax your lips into a very slight smile when you pronounce the IH sound in these words. (No English words end with the IH sound.)

grin	fifteen
liver	minister
fix	quiver
sitting	laminate

Advanced Practice

Test what you have learned in these sentences. Read the sentences once and then try repeating them using your new intonational skills.

1. The minister is finished with his sermon.

2. He had prime rib for his dinner.

3. I felt silly when he tickled me.

4. Will you pass the liver and onions, Cousin Isabel?

5. Wipe that silly grin off your face, William!

6. If I get my wish, I'll be thrilled!

7. Did you get invited to the Sweet Sixteen party?

8. It's important that you read the Declaration of Independence.

9. Ginger insists that you finish what you started.

10. Jim instills confidence in me.

The Vowel Is AY, as in TASTE

Phonetic Symbol: /e/

Keep in mind that "front vowel" refers to the location where the sound source is resonating, not where the sound is made. In other words, if you really listen, the sound AY and all other front vowels are coming from the front of your mouth.

How You Do It

To produce the AY sound, your mouth is open slightly and your lips are slightly spread. Your tongue muscles have some slight tension and your tongue tip touches the back side of your lower teeth. Having said all that, try this: the AY sound is pronounced exactly like the first letter of the alphabet.

Common Mistakes

Because this is a longer sound, you need to be careful not to cut it short. Also it's common for non-native speakers to glide upward in pitch. Remember that the sound is flat and should be delivered in monotone.

Word Practice

Practice the AY sound at the beginning of the following words. It will help if you keep thinking that the vowel sound is just like the letter *a*.

aim	apron
Amy	acorn
amiable	ace
ape	able

Practice the AY sound at the ends of these words. Note that there are several spelling combinations for the AY sound.

play	Monday
stay	sleigh
way	okay
buffet	ray

Practice the AY sound when it occurs in the middle of a word. Remember that it is a long sound; don't cut it too short.

painter	weight
table	contain
made	maintain
charade	lane

Advanced Practice

The AY sound occurs in all word positions in these practice sentences. Make certain that you pronounce each AY sound in a flat, monotone manner. Do not allow your voice to glide up to a higher pitch.

1. The baker maintained his amiable way.

2. Stay away from the table until Mom says it's okay.

3. The painter fainted when he saw his creation ruined.

4. I play games on Monday and Tuesday.

5. The box contains the remains of the drapes.

6. Amy wore a cape to the play on Friday.

7. It's a shame that Ray got paid today and lost it all.

8. Ada won the card game when she played her ace.

9. Lady bug, lady bug, fly away!

10. Aiden dressed as an angel for the school play.

The Vowel Is EH, as in TEST

Phonetic Symbol: /ɛ/

As you can see, there are very fine distinctions between the front vowels we have discussed. A slip of the tongue can quite literally result in the wrong word.

How You Do It

To produce the EH sound, your jaw drops slightly to open your mouth. Your tongue is much more relaxed compared to the tension when you produce the IH sound. Your lips are slightly spread. It is a short sound.

Common Mistakes

This may also be a new sound for new English speakers and it may take quite a bit of listening practice before you get used to it. If your tongue is not exactly on target, it can change the word entirely and cause confusion. It will help if you look at the front vowel comparison later in this chapter and keep referring to it.

Word Practice

Each of the following words begins with the short vowel sound EH. Do not stretch it out.

egg	ebony
every	else
empty	end
effort	elegant

Try pronouncing the EH sound in these words, where it occurs between other sounds.

pepper	shell
utensil	melted
ready	head
wedding	press

There are no English words that end with the EH sound.

Advanced Practice

Put what you have learned into practice by including a correct EH sound in the following sentences. Instead of reading them, try adding some conversational flair and stress key words.

1. Everyone else made an effort except Everett.

2. I can't bend my elbow or my leg.

3. Are you ready to go to the wedding, Evelyn?

4. Kelly said that my dress needed pressing.

5. Did you have eggs for breakfast again?

6. Not every story has a happy ending.

7. Jessica and her friend went shelling.

8. I had a headache so I went to bed.

9. Eddie and Jenn looked elegant.

10. The men stood at the edge of the well.

The Vowel Is A, as in ASK

Phonetic Symbol: /æ/

Some non-native English speakers can't get used to the fact that American English often calls for big, wide open sounds. You can't be shy when you speak American English!

How You Do It

Think of going to the doctor's office. The doctor says, "Open wide," as usual. Think about how that feels when you open wide. Then bring it down a bit. For the A sound, your mouth does need to be open much wider than it is for the other front vowels. Your lips are rounded, and your tongue muscles are relaxed. The tip of your tongue comes in light contact with the back of your lower teeth.

Common Mistakes

If your mouth is not open wide enough or if there is too much tension in your tongue, you might sound nasal and the quality of your voice will be affected. This is a slightly longer sound and the tone should be kept at one level. Be careful to avoid an upward swing in pitch.

Word Practice

Remember, mouth open wide on the initial sound in this group of words!

apple	Alice
alligator	animated
actress	after
ask	add

See how well you do when the A sound is in between other sounds.

bat	radical
mad	theatrical
captain	cannibal
mask	rapture

The A sound does not occur at the end of words in English.

Advanced Practice

Try practicing the A sound by saying this group of sentences. Use the intonational skills you have learned.

1. Alice is studying to be an actress in Atlanta.

2. My fat cat has a bad back.

3. The manager asked if we wanted an appetizer.

4. The cannibals acted as if they were mad, if you ask me.

5. Captain Jack was not lacking for avid admirers.

6. An apple a day can't hurt.

7. My aspiration after high school was to study agriculture.

8. Alice in Wonderland met the Mad Hatter.

9. Captain Hook was on the lookout for the alligator.

10. I'll have the rack of lamb with apple dressing.

Comparison of the Front Vowels

Track 29: I realize that the previous material has been difficult because there are only subtle sound variations and lip and tongue movements among the group. However, this section should help you because you can either compare all the vowels in relation to one another or just compare those that are troubling you. I have recorded the comparisons on the CD. By paying close attention, you'll be able to hear the subtle yet distinct differences that occur.

Important: Follow along as I pronounce the words from left to right and pay close attention to the underlined vowels and the differences in sound. Then feel how your tongue and your lips move as you go from one word to another when you say the words in each group.

EE /i/	IH /i/	AY /e/	EH /ɛ/	A /æ/
feet	fit	fate	felt	fat
meet	mitt	mate	met	mat
keep	kip	cape	kept	cap
seal	sill	sail	sell	Sally
teak	tick	take	tech	tack
peel	pill	pail	pell	pal
wheat	wit	wait	wet	wax
bean	bin	bane	Ben	ban

About the Central Vowels

The next logical step would be to discuss the central vowels, but I've decided not to include them. The reason is that I want this program to be as easy as possible for you. To include the central vowels would only cause major confusion. I'm only mentioning them in case you happened upon them in another program.

Let me explain a bit further. I have already addressed the central vowel sounds in other sections. Basically, it's the schwa sound, which we talked about in Chapter 4. It's pronounced "UH" in an unaccented syllable. In addition, the central vowels include variations of the R sound when it is preceded by a vowel. I mentioned these variations in Chapter 8 in "The Dreaded R" section. The bottom line is this: after you master the R sound as a consonant, its subtle variations will eventually come to you. To deal with them now would only cause frustration.

The Least You Need to Know

◆ Front vowels are given that name because that is where the sound resonates in the mouth.

◆ Even the smallest movement of the tongue and lips can cause a change to the entire vowel sound.

◆ Some English vowels are not part of other languages and take extra listening practice.

◆ Non-native speakers often aren't used to opening their mouths for the larger sounds of English.

Chapter 17

Watch Your Back Vowels!

In This Chapter

- ◆ Tackling the vowels essential to the American accent
- ◆ Discovering spelling varieties for identical sounds
- ◆ Learning how back vowels are unlike front vowels

The back vowels are another exciting category in the vowel family. Well, perhaps "exciting" isn't the right word, but if you want to modify a non-native accent, you have to learn to pronounce them the way Americans do. So even though they may not get your pulse racing, they are necessary and will bring you one step closer to your goal. Why are they called back vowels? Because they resonate toward the back of your mouth.

The Vowel Is OO, as in FOOD

Phonetic Symbol: /u/

This vowel is probably familiar to you and shouldn't cause much trouble. But just in case you need some extra practice, let's go through the drill.

How You Do It

The OO sound is made with the back of your tongue fairly high and the tip of your tongue pointing down. The sides of your mouth are slightly forward and your lips are rounded and slightly protruding.

Common Mistakes

This is a long sound, so be careful not to cut it short. It should be pronounced in a monotone or flat manner, so avoid sliding upward in pitch.

Word Practice

There are very few words in English that begin with this sound. I've come up with a few. See if you can add more to the practice list.

oodles	Uzi
oops	Uma
oozed	

Take note of the different spellings of this vowel sound as you practice pronouncing the correct OO sound at the ends of these words.

through	flew
zoo	true
caribou	blue
you	shoe

The most difficult pronunciation of a vowel sound is always when it's in the middle of a word. Practice saying the words in this list and remember that your lips need to be slightly protruded for this longer sound.

boot	roof
room	goofy
fool	roost
troops	drool

Advanced Practice

Keep American intonation in mind when you practice the OO vowel sound in these sentences. Again, notice the spelling variations.

1. We had oodles of noodles for dinner on Tuesday.
2. The fool threw the rusty tools from his room.
3. Captain Kangaroo was goofy but sweet.
4. Are you in the mood for fruit?
5. Would you like a blue balloon?
6. The witch flew away on her broom.
7. Did you include mushrooms in the stew?
8. I wore my boots to school.
9. As soon as you get home, go to your room.
10. Did you see *One Flew Over the Cuckoo's Nest?*

The Vowel Is UWH, as in COOK

Phonetic Symbol: /ʊ/

This is a difficult sound to hear and it may be unfamiliar to you. If you are having trouble, listen to the comparison of all the back vowels on the CD before you make an attempt to produce it yourself.

How You Do It

The UWH sound is made with the back of your tongue fairly high and your tongue tip pointing down. The sides of your mouth should be slightly forward.

Common Mistakes

Because this is a short sound, do not stretch it out. Also, your lips should not protrude or be rounded. Keep your muscles relaxed to avoid too much tension in the back of your mouth.

Word Practice

This sound appears only in the middle of English words.

cookie	hook
brook	hood
should	look
rookie	bull

Advanced Practice

Take note of how the UWH sound is spelled so you are ready when it jumps out at you. Remember, this sound occurs only in the middle of words. Practice the sentences slowly at first to get used to the correct pronunciation.

1. That rookie is a good cook.

2. Would you help me push the cookie cart?

3. I'm booking a flight to Red Hook.

4. Would you look behind the cushion?

5. Push open that wooden door with your foot.

6. Should I put sugar on this cooked cereal?

7. He hid the book in the nook.

8. I'm putting back the book that I took from the nook.

9. The crook shook as he stood in the brook.

10. My hood was under the bush at the edge of the woods.

The Vowel Is OH, as in BOAT

Phonetic Symbol: /o/

This vowel sound should be fairly easy for you. It exists in other languages, but the spellings may be different.

How You Do It

Pronounce the OH sound the same way as the name of the letter of the alphabet: *o.* Your jaw is lowered slightly and your lips are rounded and slightly puckered.

Common Mistakes

OH is a long sound and the tone needs to be flat, not gliding upward. It is important not to cut the vowel short.

Word Practice

Remember to pronounce this long sound just as you would the letter of the alphabet.

over	Ophelia
ocean	oar
odometer	obey
obese	open

When you have mastered the OH sound at the beginning of words, the next step is to practice it at the ends of words. Note the different spellings.

show	bow
glow	dough
snow	foe
piano	elbow

The OH sound occurs in the middle of each of the following words. For extra practice, develop sentences that include these words.

poker	phone
goat	folks
frozen	coax
woke	smoke

Advanced Practice

Try memorizing a few of these so it doesn't sound as if you're reading. Use some emotion and American intonation as you practice the vowel.

1. Ophelia was obese from drinking too much soda.

2. Oh, give me a home where the buffalo roam!

3. They rode on the show boat and listened to the piano.

4. The boat floated over the ocean.

5. The soldier broke his nose and elbow.

6. The goat ate Joe's frozen waffles.

7. E.T. needed to phone home.

8. My folks protested when I played poker.

9. Did you ever go to a show on opening night?

10. Moe sent me a note filled with dopey jokes.

The Vowel Is AWH, as in ALL

Phonetic Symbol: /ɔ/

This sound does not exist in any other language and could present a bit of a challenge. It calls for a big wide mouth movement. Don't worry; it will take a little practice, but you will soon get used to it.

How You Do It

To produce the AWH sound, your jaw lowers and your mouth is fairly wide. Your lips are relaxed and slightly rounded but not puckered. Your muscles are relaxed and the tip of your tongue rests just behind your lower teeth.

Common Mistakes

Putting too much tension in the back of your mouth can cause you to over-punch the sound and make it stronger than it should be. This is a long sound, so do not cut it short. The delivery is also flat and monotone, so be careful not to glide upward.

Word Practice

Relax your tongue and pronounce the AWH sound with little tension.

audience	audio
auburn	awkward
always	also
off	often

When you get to the last sound in these words, release the tension from previous sounds.

flaw	coleslaw
Macaw	jigsaw
jaw	thaw
law	paw

Make sure you are comfortable with the previous two lists before you try the next one. When the sound is in the middle of a word, it is always the most challenging.

fawn	long
because	sauce
cross	walk
calling	cough

Advanced Practice

1. It's not against the law to draw the jaw of a Macaw.

2. The audience was in awe of Audrey's auburn hair.

3. Don't put that watery sauce on my prawns.

4. It was awfully awkward for the audience when the author paused.

5. Call me cautious but I'm not breaking the law.

6. My daughter and I took a walk but didn't dawdle.

7. Austin and Claudia got caught in the auditorium.

8. I called Paula last August.

9. The officer wrote a song about being offshore for a long haul.

10. Her offspring drank strong coffee and raised ostriches.

The Vowel Is AH, as in FATHER

Phonetic Symbol: /ɑ/

There is some controversy about whether this is a back sound or a central one. The important thing is that this sound may not be familiar to you and you may have to work a bit to hear it in other people's speech before you can make it your own.

How You Do It

The AH sound requires a very big mouth movement, so don't be shy. It will take a little practice but you will soon get used to it. The tongue is low and the sound will resonate toward the back of your mouth. This is a very open sound, with your jaw lowered and your mouth open fairly wide. Your lips are slightly rounded and relaxed but be sure not to pucker them. The tongue tip rests behind the lower teeth.

Common Mistakes

Say the AH sound with as little tension as you can. Remember, it is necessary to lower your jaw and keep your mouth open wide. Relax your lips and slightly round them. Avoid giving the sound too much emphasis. Say the sound with as much ease as you can.

Word Practice

There aren't very many words that begin with the AH sound. If you encounter others, add them to your practice list.

a la mode	abandon
announce	about
agree	alone
America	away

Words that have the AH sound at the end shouldn't cause you too much difficulty if you remember it's an open, wide sound.

comma	veranda
Claudia	spa
China	idea
drama	Alabama

Although it's the most challenging, practicing the sound in a medial position will help you conquer it! Note that both *o* and *a* may represent the AH sound.

bother	corsage
father	hot
salami	calm
cot	problem

Advanced Practice

It's time to put what you've learned into action. Try using the AH sound in the following sentences. After reading them, try adding some emotion for a more conversational delivery.

1. My father said to announce that we are about to appear.
2. The pasta is on the bottom shelf.
3. Adrianna had a massage at the spa.
4. The alfalfa cannot make it to October.
5. I was shocked that the pot was so hot.
6. The monster followed the oxen.
7. The robber was odd; he stole a clock and a rock.
8. The man was looking for alms under the palm tree.
9. The Ayatollah had an opportunity for Abdul.
10. Tom dropped a pot of java.

Comparison of the Back Vowels

Just like the front vowels, the back vowels are difficult to comprehend because there are such subtle sound variations and lip and tongue movements among the group. This back vowel comparison chart should help. You can compare all the vowels in relation to one another, or just compare those that are giving you trouble. By doing so, you'll be able to hear the subtle yet distinct differences that occur.

Track 30: Important: Read the words from left to right and pay close attention to the vowels that are underlined and the differences in sound. Then feel how your tongue and lips move as you go from one word to another in each group. Also note: Words that are spelled with *oo* may have the OO sound or the UWH sound. Listen carefully!

OO /u/	UWH /ʊ/	OH /o/	AWH /ɔ/	AH /ɑ/
stool	stood	stow	stalk	stock
soon	soot	sew	saw	sock
fool	foot	foe	fought	fox
loot	look	low	lost	lot
ghoul	good	ghost	gone	got
shoe	should	show	shawl	shot

The Least You Need to Know

◆ Back vowels resonate toward the back of your mouth.

◆ Not all back vowels are familiar to non-native English speakers.

◆ The AWH sound, as in ALL, is not found in any other language.

◆ Too much overall tension can result in a vowel sounding too strong or over-punched.

Chapter 18

Diphthongs: Two for the Price of One

In This Chapter

- ◆ Hearing how vowels combine to make one sound
- ◆ Discovering why gliding is a great speech sport
- ◆ Learning why fast and flexible is the name of the game

Just when you thought you were starting to get a handle on American English vowels, another concept arises to challenge you. Meet the diphthong, a combination of two vowels pronounced as one. To explain it another way, one vowel glides into another to form one sound.

Producing diphthongs correctly is more than just know-how. Knowing how they are pronounced is one thing; actually producing them is another. When producing certain diphthongs, sometimes the journey your tongue makes is short and very controlled. For other diphthongs, your tongue has to move quite a distance in your mouth, and there may be a lot of jaw movement as well.

Because of the dialects that exist in American English, linguists argue as to how many diphthongs there actually are, and they categorize them differently. For our purposes, we will stick with the diphthongs of standard American English.

The Diphthong Is OW, as in OUT

Phonetic Symbol: /aʊ/

The two partners that join to say OW are AH and OO. If you can quickly glide the two of them together, you have just experienced success. If you don't get it at first, you will with a little listening and practice. Just remember that AH and OO are not equal partners. The main emphasis is on the first sound—the AH sound.

How You Do It

Your jaw lowers to open your mouth, and your lips are relaxed and rounded a little bit. Your muscles are also relaxed and the tongue tip is placed behind the gum line of the lower teeth. Keep in mind that it's a longer sound produced by first saying AH and then gliding down to a lower OO. Your lips become more puckered along the way.

Common Mistakes

This is a longer sound, so be careful not to cut it short. Remember that this is a two-step process, with the first sound getting more emphasis. Be careful not to tighten your muscles. Just relax and let the glide happen. Think of someone pinching you. What would you say? OW!

Listening Practice

Track 31: The two sounds that join to create the diphthong OW are AH and OO … OW. If it seems difficult for you, listening will help. First listen, and then repeat after me.

Beginning:	outer	ounce	ouch	owl
Middle:	hound	noun	house	sour
End:	endow	plow	vow	allow

Here's the Drill: OW

As you practice this diphthong when it occurs at the beginning of words, be aware of changing your mouth position. But it has to be fast!

outrage	ouch
outcome	outer
Audi	oust
ourselves	outburst

Practice these words in which the diphthong occurs at the end. Make a special note of the differences in spellings.

allow	how
endow	Mao
brow	sow
bough	chow

When the diphthong occurs in the middle of a word, it may take a special effort to produce the sound correctly.

shower	lousy
cloud	house
mound	mountain
flounder	towel

Advanced Practice

I've done the hard part for you by underlining the words with the OW diphthong. You do the rest by practicing.

1. Every h<u>ou</u>r he pr<u>ow</u>led through the cr<u>ow</u>d.

2. The <u>ow</u>l on the b<u>ough</u> weighed 16 <u>ou</u>nces.

3. I was <u>ou</u>traged when he pl<u>ow</u>ed into my <u>Au</u>di.

4. Ab<u>ou</u>t h<u>ow</u> many h<u>ou</u>rs will we be <u>ou</u>tside?

5. Did you c<u>ou</u>nt the fl<u>ow</u>ers?

6 H<u>ow</u> did you get the br<u>ow</u>n c<u>ow</u> to wear a cr<u>ow</u>n?

7. There was a br<u>ow</u>n fl<u>ou</u>nder in a shop in t<u>ow</u>n.

8. The cl<u>ow</u>n had a lot of cl<u>ou</u>t in the r<u>ou</u>nd tent.

9. There is no d<u>ou</u>bt, we must control <u>ou</u>rselves and not get l<u>ou</u>d.

10. There were cl<u>ou</u>ds ar<u>ou</u>nd the m<u>ou</u>ntaintop, so the view did not am<u>ou</u>nt to much.

The Diphthong Is AYE, as in EYE

Phonetic Symbol: /ɑɪ/

This diphthong is a smooth-moving combination of the vowel sounds AH as in *father* and EE as in *me*. If you practice them together fast enough, the sound should be fairly easy to conquer.

How You Do It

Lower your jaw to open your mouth, and keep your lips rounded; do not pucker them. The muscles are relaxed and the tongue tip touches the back of your lower teeth. Think of the letter *i* in the alphabet.

Common Mistakes

Once again, you need to be cautious and keep in mind that although the sound is long in duration, it needs to be delivered without an upward glide in pitch.

Listening Practice

Track 32: Listen as I glide the two sounds AH and EE together to make AYE. First listen and then repeat after me.

Beginning:	aisle	isolate	idea	ivy
Middle:	trying	rice	night	criteria
End:	sky	defy	comply	justify

Here's the Drill: AYE

The following provides practice for the AYE sound when it is the first sound that occurs in a word.

ice	isolated
Einstein	idea
Idaho	island
I'll	item

Now practice saying these words that have the AYE sound at the end. Notice the different letters and combinations of letters that represent the AYE sound.

defy	lie
supply	high
why	rye
alibi	sigh

Remember the greater emphasis is on the first part of AYE. Here's your middle-of-the-word list.

mighty	rice
title	sublime
criteria	shine
lime	behind

Advanced Practice

You can't tell how really well you are doing until you practice the sound in sentences and conversational speech. Give these a try.

1. Why don't you comply with my client's idea?

2. Irene was whining, and Diane was irate.

3. Brian said a final goodbye to his driver.

4. I like the limes served on the lanai at night.

5. The pilot didn't fly over the isolated island that Friday.

6. Some say she's wild, but I think she's quite nice.

7. Cheyenne used to be shy when she talked to a guy.

8. I plan to gripe if they don't comply.

9. I'm going to get new designer eyeglasses.

10. Key lime is my favorite kind of pie.

The Diphthong Is OY, as in BOY

Phonetic Symbol: /ɔɪ/

This time you will be gliding from the AWH as in *all* to the EE as in *eat*. It takes a pretty fast move to pull it off.

How You Do It

Lower your jaw so your mouth is open. Your tongue muscles are relaxed and the tip of your tongue rests behind the lower teeth. Keep in mind that this is a longer sound and that there's no swing upward in pitch.

Common Mistakes

Avoid creating too much tension in the back of your mouth. Relaxing the speech muscles will help. Keep the emphasis on the beginning of the sound and keep your delivery pitch flat.

Listening Practice

Track 33: Listen to the word examples as I glide AWH and EE together to create the OY sound.

Beginning:	oil	oyster	oink	oily
Middle:	broil	loin	choice	coin
End:	destroy	employ	annoy	enjoy

Here's the Drill: OY

Practice saying these words to perfect the OY sound at the beginning.

oil	ointment
oily	oilcloth
oyster	oink
oiler	oilskin

End-of-the-word practice will help build your skills and make using the correct sound more habitual.

annoy	joy
decoy	deploy
destroy	alloy
employ	Roy

The OY sound can be spelled two ways, *oy* and *oi*.

sirloin	moist
paranoid	broil
voyage	soil
coin	loyal

Advanced Practice

If you are ready to incorporate the OY sound in sentences, here are some to challenge you. Remember your intonation!

1. The sirloin was moist even though it was broiled.

2. My employer was annoyed, but I was overjoyed.

3. They deployed the fleet, which was destroyed.

4. The annoying boy enjoyed the noisy toys.

5. Joyce joined us at the burger joint.

6. I recoiled when I read that they were boiled in oil!

7. He used his coins to buy a few cowboy toys.

8. The poisonous snake was coiled on top of the moist soil.

9. The boy's ploy was to use a decoy.

10. If you have a choice, avoid Roy's singing voice.

The Diphthong Is IU, as in YOU

Phonetic Symbol: /iu/

If you take a close look at the phonetic symbol, you can see that this diphthong is a combination of EE and OO.

How You Do It

Your lips travel forward to produce this sound. Your mouth is open slightly, and the muscles are a little tense. The tongue tip is right behind the lower teeth. Initially you will produce EE and quickly glide to OO. It is pronounced the same way as the letter *u* in the alphabet.

Common Mistakes

As with many vowels, there's a tendency to shorten the sound and change the pitch upward. This is a long sound delivered without any change in pitch.

Listening Practice

Track 34: If you listen closely, you can hear that this diphthong is a combination of the EE and OO sounds.

Beginning:	youth	union	universal	unique
Middle:	puberty	beautiful	mutant	refuse
End:	view	hue	few	cue

Here's the Drill: IU

Practice the diphthong in the initial position in the following words. For extra practice, put each word in a sentence, using the principles of American intonation.

union	uniform
unique	universal
unit	usual
used	Yukon

Notice the different letter combinations that stand for the IU sound when the sound occurs at the end of a word.

few	mew
menu	queue
cue	view
hue	review

When the sound is preceded by other sounds, you need to glide into it. But remember not to cut it short.

huge	beauty
mule	refuse
music	fewer
January	puberty

Advanced Practice

When you can practice the target sound in a sentence without any difficulty, make the transfer into your conversational speech.

1. Hugh went to church and sat in the pew.

2. The beautiful woman refused to date Hubert.

3. I usually wear my uniform and carry my bugle.

4. Did you go to the Yukon for the view?

5. A university education is valuable for your future.

6. The mute mule was born in Cuba.

7. He would never refuse a good Cuban cigar.

8. He lost his sense of humor when he reached puberty.

9. As usual, I need a huge favor from you.

10. Here are a few cubes of sugar for you.

The Least You Need to Know

◆ A diphthong is a combination of two vowels that blend into one sound.

◆ The emphasis is always on the first part of a diphthong.

◆ Mastering diphthongs takes excellent muscle coordination and fluid movement.

◆ Different American dialects have different diphthongs.

Appendix A

Glossary

accent   The way a person sounds when speaking a particular language.

air stream   The flow of the air used in speech.

articulation   The act of producing a speech sound.

articulators   The physical structures that produce speech sounds, including the tongue, lips, hard palate, soft palate, and teeth.

carryover   Applying newly learned speech patterns in conversation.

consonants   Speech sounds that are constricted by any of the articulators.

content words   Words that are vital to convey meaning.

diphthongs   A vowel that glides into another vowel to form one sound.

function words   Words that link content words.

glide   A smooth movement of speech.

hard palate   The anterior bony portion on the roof of the mouth.

intelligibility   The degree to which speech is understandable.

intonation   The rhythm and melody of a language.

larynx   The structure containing the vocal cords; also referred to as the voice box.

linking   The connection of sounds between adjacent words.

phoneme   The smallest possible unit of sound.

pitch   The voice tone used in speech.

schwa   A neutral vowel sound typically occurring in unstressed syllables.

soft palate   The fleshy portion on the roof of the mouth.

speech triggers   Situational reminders to use corrected speech habits in real-life scenarios.

stress   The emphasis given to a specific syllable or word by increasing its loudness, length, or pitch.

syllable   A unit of pronunciation having one vowel sound.

uvula   The small, fleshy conical body that projects downward from the soft palate.

vocal cords   Membranes found in the larynx, or voice box.

voiced consonant   A consonant sound produced as the vocal cords vibrate.

voiceless consonant   A consonant sound produced without the vibration of the vocal cords.

vowel   A speech sound unobstructed by any articulators.

Appendix B

Recording Your Speech Sample

The following paragraph contains all the sounds of the English language. As explained in Chapter 2, you should record this sample before you begin to work on modifying your accent. Then compare it to the model on the CD. Recording the paragraph on a regular basis will help you monitor your progress. Although this is not an expert analysis, it will give you a general idea of the sounds you need to target and perhaps some insight about your intonation. If you would like a professional analysis of your speech by an accent reduction specialist, consult the resources in Appendix D.

> **Track 1:** Please call Stella. Ask her to bring these things with her from the store: six spoons of fresh snow peas, five thick slabs of blue cheese, and maybe a snack for her brother Bob. We also need a small plastic snake and a big toy frog for the kids. She can scoop these things into three red bags, and we will go meet her Wednesday at the train station.

Ask yourself these questions as you compare your recorded speech sample to the one on the CD:

1. Did you substitute any other sounds for the ones that were spoken?

2. Did you add additional sounds to any words?

3. Did you omit sounds that should have been there, especially at the ends of words?

4. Do your vowels sound the same as on the CD sample?

5. Listen to your intonation. Was your delivery choppy? Was it monotone?

6. Think about your pitch. Was it high or low?

7. Consider your rate of speech. How does it compare to the sample?

Permission to use the previous sample was given by Steven H. Weinberger, Associate Professor and Director of Linguistics in the Department of English at George Mason University.

Speech Habits by Nationality

This information is based, in part, on the 25 years of original research of Paul Shoebottom, Instructor in Upper School ESL (English as a Second Language) at the Frankfurt International School in Frankfurt, Germany.

Arabic

There are about three times as many vowels in English as there are in Arabic. Many Arabic speakers of English are unable to hear and/or pronounce these unfamiliar vowels, especially in words with subtle vowel differences. For example, they may not be able to distinguish between the vowel sounds in these pairs of words: *ship* and *sheep*, *bad* and *bed*, *bit* and *bet*.

Problems in pronouncing consonants include the inability to produce the voiceless th and voiced TH sounds. Words such as *thin* and *this* are often pronounced as "sin" and "zis." Other sound substitutions include using the B sound for P in the initial position and the F sound for V.

Consonant clusters (two or more consonant sounds together) are also troublesome, and the Arabic speaker often adds an extra vowel between consonants. For example, *closet* becomes "cuh-loset." Other sound errors include using the SH sound in place of CH, ZH, and DJ. Speakers may also produce a throaty H sound, which is not part of English.

Regarding intonation, Arabic speakers have difficulty with the seemingly random stress pattern of English and tend to pronounce all sounds rather than adopting the American habit of stressing some sounds and words and "swallowing" others. A throaty hesitation or "stop" before initial vowels contributes to choppy intonation.

Chinese

There are many Chinese dialects, including Wu, Cantonese, and Taiwanese. There is no single Chinese language. Northern Chinese, known as Mandarin, is the mother tongue of about 70 percent of Chinese speakers.

The English sound system is difficult for native Chinese speakers because some English phonemes (simple sounds) do not exist in Chinese. Stress and intonation patterns are also different. Chinese is a tonal language, meaning that it uses pitch to distinguish different word meanings. In English, changes in pitch are used to emphasize a thought or express emotion, not to differentiate words.

Chinese speakers have trouble with English vowels and diphthongs (two vowels spoken as one), and are unable to hear differences in words such as *ship* and *sheep*, *it* and *eat*, *full* and *fool*. They also have trouble distinguishing the difference between the R and L sounds. This explains why *rake* and *rice* might be pronounced as "lake" and "lice." Because ending words with consonants is unusual in Chinese, final consonants are often omitted or an extra vowel is added to the end of words.

Dutch

Because the Dutch and English sound systems are similar, Dutch native speakers have fewer problems understanding and producing spoken English than many others. Some confusion of English vowel sounds still may occur, especially in close vowel sounds as demonstrated in words such as *sit* and *seat*, *set* and *sat*, *not* and *nut*, *caught* and *coat*.

Words that end in voiced consonants are not part of the Dutch language. These words would be pronounced with their voiceless counterpart. For example, *rub* would be pronounced as "rup" and *bird* as "birt." Another tendency is substituting the V sound for W. Voiced and voiceless TH also cause difficulty. *Think* may be pronounced as "sink" or "tink"; *than* may become "dan."

The stress and intonation patterns in Dutch and English are similar, although Dutch speakers have a tendency to emphasize words that American English speakers reduce or minimize.

French

French speakers of English have difficulty hearing the difference between words where the only difference is the vowel. For example, it is difficult for French speakers to distinguish between word pairs such as these: *ship* and *sheep*, *live* and *leave*, *full* and *fool*. Another common problem has to do with voiced and voiceless TH. *Think*, for example, might be pronounced "sink," and *then* might be "zen." Omitting the H sound at the beginning of words is another tendency because the sound does not exist in French.

The stress patterns of English are quite different from those of French. When French speakers naturally apply their own stress patterns to English, the result is a choppy intonation pattern.

German

The sounds of English and German are similar, as are stress and intonation patterns. However, the voiced and voiceless TH sound in words such as *the* and *thing* does not exist in German, and many speakers have problems producing them correctly. German words beginning with *w* are pronounced with a V sound. This explains the mispronunciation of English words such as *we* or *wine* as "ve" and "vine."

Hebrew

Hebrew has many fewer vowels than English, and no diphthongs. Speakers have difficulty differentiating long and short vowels which causes mispronunciation of words such as *ship* and *sheep* or *bet* and *bit*. As with many English learners, native Hebrew speakers struggle with the voiced and voiceless TH as well as pronouncing a clear L sound. They may also have difficulties with the W and V sounds, pronouncing *vine* as "wine," or vice versa.

American intonation is also difficult for Hebrew speakers due to their pattern of stressing the last or next to last syllable in words. In English, stress on syllables is more random. A throaty delivery of certain sounds is obvious to an American listener.

Hindi/Urdu

Hindi and Urdu are the national languages of India and Pakistan, respectively. When they are spoken, the languages are virtually identical, but not in their written form.

In comparison with English, Hindi has approximately half as many vowels and twice as many consonants. This leads to several problems of pronunciation. One difficulty is distinguishing phonemes in words such as *said* and *sad*, *par* and *paw*, *vet* and *wet*, and so on. Words containing the letters *th* (*this*, *thing*, *months*) will cause Hindi learners the same kind of problems that they cause most other learners of English. The ZH sound, represented by the *s* in *pleasure* is missing in Hindi, so pronunciation of such words is difficult. Consonant clusters at the beginning or end of words are more common in English than in Hindi. This leads to errors in the pronunciation of words such as *straight* ("istraight"), *fly* ("faly"), and *film* ("filam").

In Hindi/Urdu, stress is accomplished by significant rises in voice pitch rather than by the heavier articulation that typifies English stress. Speakers have difficulty with the irregular pattern of English stress and tend to give equal weight to all words. The result is the "sing-song" effect as perceived by native English speakers.

Italian

Italian speakers of English typically have problems hearing and pronouncing subtle differences in vowels. For example, *cot* and *coat*, *ship* and *sheet*. Also difficult for Italian speakers of English is the H sound, which is usually omitted in words such as *hotel*, *hill*, or *house*. Conversely, Italian speakers may add an *h* to words beginning with a vowel. Because many Italian words end with a vowel, Italian speakers of English may add a short vowel sound to the end of English words that end with a consonant.

As with most languages, problems arise with the voiceless th sound. Speakers may substitute a T or D sound instead. Many Italian speakers also trill or roll the R sound, in stark contrast to the American English sound. Another habit is to voice the *g* in the NG sound, resulting in "sing-ger," which rhymes with *finger*. There is also a tendency to pronounce all English syllables and words with equal emphasis, unlike the American English intonational pattern.

Japanese

Japanese has only five pure vowel sounds that may be short or long. The syllable structure is simple, generally with the vowel sound preceded by one of approximately 15 consonant sounds. By comparison, English is much more complex and difficult for Japanese speakers to perceive and pronounce. Consonant combinations pose special problems, and Japanese native speakers often insert short vowels between consonants. Problems also occur in pronouncing diphthongs.

The most noticeable problem with consonants is seen in the inability to differentiate between the L and R sounds. Words such as *lot* and *rot* or *lake* and *rake* are difficult for some to pronounce correctly. Other problems include pronouncing the V sound as B (so, *van* would come out as "ban" and *very* as "berry"). And finally, the voiced and voiceless TH are unfamiliar to speakers of other languages.

Korean

Unlike English, Korean is a syllable-timed language in which individual word stress plays no part. This is radically different from English and accounts for the flat or monotone quality of a Korean speaker of English.

Because several English consonants do not exist in Korean, the primary difficulty arises in the production of those sounds. The most significant of these are the voiceless and voiced TH in words such as *thin*, *through*, *then*, and *this*. Korean speakers make other sound substitutions as well, including the B sound for V. And they have trouble distinguishing between the R and L sounds. Differences in syllable structure between the two languages may lead to the addition of a short vowel sound at the end of English words. Short vowels may also be lengthened.

Russian

The Russian vowel system contains only five vowels and there is no differentiation between long and short vowels, an obvious contrast from the extensive vowel and diphthong system of English. Unfamiliarity with vowel sounds leads to difficulty in distinguishing between and correctly pronouncing such word pairs as *sat* and *set* or *sit* and *seat*.

The TH sound does not exist in Russian, so words such as *thin*, *there*, and *clothes* are difficult. As with many other learners of English, the W and V sounds are troublesome, with *west* being pronounced "vest," for example, or vice versa. The NG sound at the end of words such as *sing* or *thinking* is difficult for Russian speakers to produce accurately and is often omitted. So, for example, *thinking* would end up as "thinkin."

As with English, Russian has variable stress patterns. However Russian speakers may give weight to words that English speakers minimize. Russian learners may ask questions with falling instead of rising intonation.

Spanish

English has a wider and more complicated vowel sound system than Spanish does. Therefore, Spanish speakers have difficulty producing or even perceiving the various English vowel sounds. Specific problems include the failure to distinguish the different sounds in words such as *ship* and *sheep*, *taught* and *tot*, and *fool* and *full*.

Producing English consonant sounds is not as problematic for many Spanish learners, but they may have problems in the following aspects:

1. Not pronouncing final consonants accurately or strong enough: "cart" for *card*, "brish" for *bridge*; "thing" for *think*.

2. A tendency to add the prefix "eh" to some words beginning with *s*, especially when *s* is followed by another consonant. For example, *school* becomes "eh-school" and *strip* becomes "eh-strip."

3. Omitting some sounds when consonants are together. For example, *next* becomes "nes" and *instead* becomes "istead."

4. Substituting the DJ sound for the Y sound, saying "jess" for *yes*.

American intonation can be difficult for a native Spanish speaker. Spanish is a syllable-timed language and English is a stress-timed language. Meaning or information usually conveyed in English by the combination of stress, pitch, and rhythm is not part of Spanish intonation and must be learned.

Swedish

Like English, Swedish is a stress-timed language with similar intonation patterns. However, some minor words that Americans "swallow" or minimize, such as *like*, *but*, *the*, and *was* may sound overstressed to the American ear. Unlike English, Swedish is a tone language, meaning that differences in pitch can change word meanings. This may result in some sentences ending in an upward pitch, as if asking a question.

As far as pronunciation, there are many sound similarities with both languages. However, Swedish speakers may have difficulty differentiating the vowels in word pairs such as *ship* and *sheep* or *bed* and *bad*. Although there is considerable overlap of consonants between English and Swedish, as with many other languages, correct pronunciation of voiced and voiceless TH is problematic. Another tendency is to substitute the SH sound for ZH and the S sound for Z.

Vietnamese

There are many sound and intonation differences between Vietnamese and English. Vietnamese is a tonal language, unlike English, and native speakers have difficulty with the American English pattern of syllable and word stress, often speaking English in a monotone or flat manner.

Vietnamese have difficulty distinguishing between long and short vowels, or they add an extra vowel sound between consonants. Speakers may not produce final consonants because there are fewer final consonants in Vietnamese and those that do exist have a different tonal quality than English. Sound substitutions are frequent and native Vietnamese speakers need to focus on most vowels and consonants of the English language.

Appendix D

Resources and References

American English Dictionaries with Phonetic Symbols

- www.yourdictionary.com
- www.dictionary.com

American English Talking Dictionaries:

- www.howjsay.com
- www.cooldictionary.com
- http://aruljohn.com/voice.pl

American English Visual and Audio Demonstration

♦ www.uiowa.edu/~acadtech/phonetics/#

♦ www.uiowa.edu/~acadtech/phonetics/english/frameset.html

A collaborative effort of the Departments of Spanish and Portuguese, German, Speech Pathology and Audiology, and the Academic Technologies at the University of Iowa.

The International Phonetic Alphabet (IPA)

♦ www.langsci.ucl.ac.uk/ipa   Home of the IPA.

♦ www.omniglot.com/writing/ipa.htm   Omniglot: Written systems and languages of the world.

♦ www.antimoon.com/how/pronunc-soundsipa.htm   IPA printable charts.

Active Listening Resources

♦ www.manythings.org/listen   Professionally recorded stories with text so you can listen and read along.

♦ www.gutenberg.org   Project Gutenberg; follow the link to the audio books section.

♦ www.englishlistening.com   The English Listening Lounge; a collection of authentic listening opportunities based on your proficiency level.

♦ www.npr.org/programs   National Public Radio (NPR) Online; news and feature stories.

♦ www.voanews.com/specialenglish   Voice of America Special English Program; a program designed especially for new English speakers; live newscasts and recorded feature stories delivered at a slow pace without idioms.

Speech Habits of Specific Nationalities

♦ www.btinternet.com/~ted.power/phono.html   Ted Power's English Language Learning and Teaching; major resource for the speech habits of people from numerous countries as compared to British English.

♦ http://esl.fis.edu/grammar/langdiff/index.htm   ESL Department of the Frankfurt International School in Frankfurt, Germany.

Speech Accent Archive

♦ http://accent.gmu.edu   An opportunity to contribute to the speech sample archive and participate in a study by George Mason University that compares the demographic and linguistic backgrounds of speakers to determine which variables are key predictors of each accent.

Professional Resources

For a more in-depth evaluation of your accent:

♦ www.accentonspeaking.com   Accent on Speaking—Sheri Summers.

References

Chwat, Sam. *Living Language Speak Up! Accent Elimination Program*. New York: Living Language (editions specific to different native languages published in various years).

Cook, Ann. *American Accent Training*. Hauppauge, NY: Barron's Educational Series, 2000.

Lujan, Beverly A. *The American Accent Guide: A Complete and Comprehensive Course on American English Pronunciation for Individuals of All Language Backgrounds*. Salt Lake City, UT: Lingual Arts Publishers, 2004.

Peterson, Elizabeth. *Accent Reduction 101: A Complete Program to Improve American and Career Speech for Busy Professionals on the Go!*. Aurora, CO: Speech and Voice Enterprises, 2008.

Stern, David Allen. *The Sound & Style of American English*. Lyndonville, VT: Dialect Accent Specialists, 2006.

Summers, Sheri. *The American Accent Workshop*. www.accentworkshop. com.

Index